KT-561-107

CONTENTS

KEY FACTS

CONTRACT LAW

SECOND EDITION

CHRIS TURNER

Hodder Arnold

A MEMBER OF THE HODDER HEADLINE GROUP

Orders: please contact Bookpoint Ltd, 130 Milton Park, Abingdon, Oxon OX14 4SB.
Telephone: (44) 01235 827720. Fax: (44) 01235 400454. Lines are open from 9.00–6.00,
Monday to Saturday, with a 24-hour message answering service.
You can also order through our website: www.hoddereducation.co.uk

British Library Cataloguing in Publication Data
A catalogue record for this title is available from The British Library.

ISBN-10: 0 340 88949 7
ISBN-13: 978 0 340 88949 7

First published 2001
Second Edition 2005
Impression number   10 9 8 7 6 5 4 3 2 1
Year   2008 2007 2006 2005

Cover design by Stewart Larking
Typeset by Transet Limited, Coventry, England.
Printed in Great Britain for Hodder Arnold, an imprint of Hodder Education, a member of the
Hodder Headline Group, 338 Euston Road, London NW1 3BH by Cox & Wyman Ltd,
Reading, Berks.

PREFACE

The Key Facts series is designed to give a clear view of each subject. This will be useful to students when tackling new topics and is invaluable as a revision aid. Most chapters open with an outline in diagram form of the points covered in that chapter. The points are then developed in list form to make learning easier. Supporting cases are given throughout by name and for some complex areas the facts of cases are given to reinforce the point being made.

Some areas of contract law are very complex and this book helps students by breaking down each topic into key points. This is done for both the important general principles as well as for specific areas. The topics covered make it a useful resource for contract law components of degree courses, ILEX courses and A level specifications.

The law is stated as I believe it to be at 1st January 2005.

CHAPTER 1
FUNDAMENTALS OF CONTRACT LAW

1.1 THE ORIGINS AND FUNCTIONS OF CONTRACT LAW

1.1.1 The origins of the law of contract

1. The origins of the law of contract are often associated with the nineteenth-century period of *laissez faire* economics.
2. Contract law also has origins in the law of the Middle Ages.
3. Modern contract law really begins with the need to differentiate between formal and informal arrangements between parties.
4. Traditionally all formal agreements, e.g. transfers of land, were under seal, and proof of the agreement was the deed itself.
5. Informal agreements might be written but were more commonly oral, with the consequent difficulty of proof.
6. Outside of property law, two types of formal agreement were recognised as early as the twelfth century.

   - Covenant – an agreement to do a specific act, e.g. erect a building on land, and specific performance was possible.
   - Debt – an agreement to pay a sum of money; the remedy would be the payment of the debt.

7. Informal agreements were called 'parol' agreements, having no formal proof of their existence and based on word of honour.
8. The major actions identified in the early law were:

   - debt – e.g. an informal (oral) agreement to sell goods; the action would generally be for the price of the goods;
   - detinue – a claim for a chattel due, e.g. an undelivered horse.

9. By the fourteenth century the courts had developed the action of assumpsit. This developed out of the tort of trespass and derived from the writ action 'on the case' – an adaptation of the writ to specific circumstances of the case. It was in effect an action for breach of an informal promise. The assumpsit was the undertaking to carry out the promise.

10. In the sixteenth century the problems of proof in relation to parol agreements led to the development of a doctrine of consideration.

11. In the nineteenth century many of the basic rules were developed and influenced by *laissez faire* attitudes.

12. Many basic principles have subsequently been modified by common law once discovered to be unworkable.

13. A move to consumer protection in the late twentieth century, and the influence of membership of the European Union, have been responsible for some drastic modifications.

1.1.2 What is a contract?

1. A contract is an agreement between two parties by which both are bound in law and which can therefore be enforced in a court or other equivalent forum.

2. Contracts are distinguished from agreements, which are not binding, and from promises, which are enforceable but unilateral.

   - To be enforceable a contractual agreement must be based on mutuality of intent – no mutuality, no contract.
   - Proof of the existence of the agreement is usually needed, based on the idea that a person will not give up goods or services without a payment in return.
   - Some agreements give rise to legal relations, some do not.
   - A contract is an agreement based on the promises of two parties; a will is a binding promise but is one-sided.

1.1.3 Why contracts are enforced

1. Contract law is important as it is a way of regulating relationships – we can safely make arrangements with other people if we know those agreements have the force of law.

2. So, contractual arrangements are enforced for three specific reasons:

- because they create legitimate expectations in both parties that their undertakings will be carried out;
- because it is quite common for a party to a contract to incur further expenditure on reliance on the promise made;
- because if one party actually does perform his/her side of the bargain it would be unconscionable to allow the other party to avoid paying the price.

1.2 FREEDOM OF CONTRACT

1. Many rules of contract law developed in the nineteenth century under the doctrine of *laissez faire* economics, when the idea also developed that parties to a contract should be free to negotiate any terms they wish to be in the contract.

2. Common law has generally tried to follow this principle and to give effect to the wishes of the parties.

3. However, there are many problems with freedom of contract:

- inequality of bargaining strength of the two parties;
- the acceptance of implied terms;
- the use of standard form contracts;
- statutory intervention to protect consumers;
- the obligation to implement EU law.

4. Thus, freedom of contract is not straightforward, and parties may need to be aware of contractual obligations that they must comply with but which they have not chosen themselves.

CHAPTER 2

FORMATION OF A CONTRACT

2.1 FORMATION OF CONTRACTS

1. The first stage in any contractual dispute is to establish if a contract actually exists. This depends on proper formation.

2. There are three key ingredients to formation:

   - agreement – based on mutuality over the terms, agreement exists when a valid acceptance follows a valid offer;
   - consideration – given by both sides, the *quid pro quo*, and the proof that the bargain exists;
   - intention to create legal relations – since a contract is legally enforceable, unlike mere gratuitous promises.

3. Other factors affecting formation include:

   - form – the way the contract is created, e.g. sales of land can only be made in the form of a deed. Form is an issue with speciality contracts but not with simple contracts;
   - capacity – the ability of one party to enter a contract and of the other party to enforce it, e.g. to protect minors;
   - privity of contract and the rights of third parties – generally a contract is only enforceable by or against a party to it, subject to exceptions, and certain third party rights are now protected in the Contracts (Rights of Third Parties) Act 1999.

4. The rules were devised when contractual relationships were less sophisticated and often now seem inappropriate e.g.:

   - vending machines – (*Thornton v Shoe Lane Parking* (1971));
   - standard form contracts – in (*Butler Machine Tool Co. Ltd. v Ex-Cell-O Corporation* (1979)). Lord Denning suggested that we should determine whether a contract exists by examining all the appropriate evidence rather than being limited by the simple rules –few judges would support him.

5. The existence of an agreement is measured objectively in English law, and so is as much to do with the surrounding

factual circumstances as it is to do with the state of mind of either party.

6. Judges have strained the basic principles in order to find consideration to enforce promises that they believe are made in a context that should make them binding.

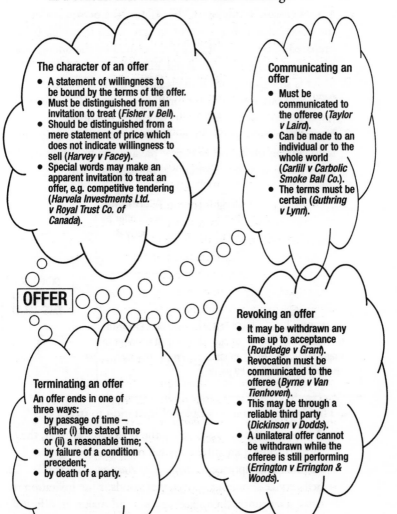

The character of an offer

- A statement of willingness to be bound by the terms of the offer.
- Must be distinguished from an invitation to treat (*Fisher v Bell*).
- Should be distinguished from a mere statement of price which does not indicate willingness to sell (*Harvey v Facey*).
- Special words may make an apparent invitation to treat an offer, e.g. competitive tendering (*Harvela Investments Ltd. v Royal Trust Co. of Canada*).

Communicating an offer

- Must be communicated to the offeree (*Taylor v Laird*).
- Can be made to an individual or to the whole world (*Carlill v Carbolic Smoke Ball Co.*).
- The terms must be certain (*Guthring v Lynn*).

OFFER

Terminating an offer

An offer ends in one of three ways:
- by passage of time – either (i) the stated time or (ii) a reasonable time;
- by failure of a condition precedent;
- by death of a party.

Revoking an offer

- It may be withdrawn any time up to acceptance (*Routledge v Grant*).
- Revocation must be communicated to the offeree (*Byrne v Van Tienhoven*).
- This may be through a reliable third party (*Dickinson v Dodds*).
- A unilateral offer cannot be withdrawn while the offeree is still performing (*Errington v Errington & Woods*).

2.2 OFFER

2.2.1 The character of an offer

1. A contract usually begins with acceptance of an offer. An offer is a statement by one party, the offeror (the person making the offer), identifying terms of an agreement by which (s)he is prepared to be bound if they are accepted by the offeree (the person to whom the offer is made).

2. Offer is straightforward if made in the form of a question: 'Will you buy my law book for the price stated?' – offeree responds positively and accepts or rejects the offer.

3. Not all contracts begin as simply. Often an offer is only made following an invitation to treat – passive conduct inviting the other party to make an offer, e.g. in diagram form:

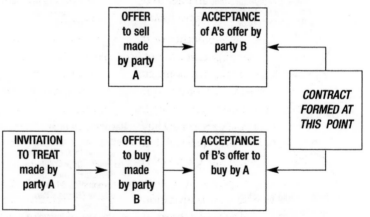

4. There are numerous examples of invitation to treat.

- Auctions – the lot displayed is the invitation to treat, the individual bids are offers, the fall of the auctioneer's hammer is acceptance – (*British Car Auctions v Wright* (1972)).
- Self-service shopping – display of goods is the invitation to treat, a customer then selects goods and makes an offer to buy at the checkout, which is then accepted or not by the shopkeeper – (*Pharmaceutical Society of Great Britain v Boots Cash Chemists Ltd.* (1953)).

- The same applies to goods displayed in shop windows (*Fisher v Bell* (1961)) on whether display of a flick knife was unlawful under the Offensive Weapons Act.
- Advertisements – the advertisement is the invitation to which a person responds by making an offer to buy (*Partridge v Crittenden* (1968)).
- Catalogues, as for auctions, so a lot can be withdrawn without any consequences (*Harris v Nickerson* (1873)).
- Invitations to council tenants to buy their council houses and flats (*Gibson v Manchester City Council* (1979)).
- Tenders to provide goods or services – invitations to suppliers to offer a particular price for which they will provide the goods or services; the party inviting bids then selects a bid (*Spencer v Harding* (1870)).
- Mere statement of price – merely stating an acceptable price does not make it an offer to sell; the other party must still offer to buy at the price (*Harvey v Facey* (1893)).

5. In all cases the significance of the invitation to treat is that the person responding to it has not accepted an offer, so their action does not at that point create a binding contract.
6. Sometimes precise wording is more important than context. While something seems more like an invitation to treat it may in fact have the effect of an offer, so that a positive response by the other party may well lead to a contract being formed.
7. The wording limits the people capable of responding.
   (a) Unilateral offers, i.e. contained in advertisements, and otherwise seen as invitations to treat, e.g. rewards. An offeree is already defined in the reward (the person who complies with its terms) so that the person need not make any offer to comply, they merely carry out the stated task (*Carlill v Carbolic Smoke Ball Co.* (1893)).
   (b) A statement of price made during negotiations indicating that an offer exists (*Bigg v Boyd Gibbins* (1971)).
   (c) Competitive tendering, i.e. stating that the contract will be given to the bidder making the highest (or lowest) bid, in which case only that person can form the contract, and they accept by making the highest or lowest bid (*Harvela*

Investments Ltd. v Royal Trust Co. of Canada (1985)).
Competitive tendering also means that parties entering
bids may have them considered (*Blackpool & Fylde Aero
Club v Blackpool Borough Council* (1990)).

2.2.2 Communication of offers

1. A valid offer must be communicated to the offeree. It would
   be unfair for a person to be bound by an offer of which (s)he
   had no knowledge (*Taylor v Laird* (1856)).
2. So the offeree must have clear knowledge of the existence of
   an offer for it to be enforceable (*Inland Revenue Commissioners
   v Fry* (2001)).
3. An offer can be made to one individual, but also to the whole
   world, when the offer can be accepted by any party who had
   genuine notice of it (*Carlill v Carbolic Smoke Ball Co.* (1893)).
4. The terms of the offer must be certain. The parties must
   know in advance what they are contracting over, so any vague
   words may invalidate the agreement (*Guthing v Lynn* (1831)).

2.2.3 Revocation of offers

1. Revocation refers to the withdrawal of an offer.
2. An offeror may withdraw the offer any time before the offeree
   has accepted it (*Routledge v Grant* (1828)). It would be unfair
   to expect the offeror to wait indefinitely for an offeree's response.
3. An offer made in response to an invitation to treat may also
   be withdrawn if not yet accepted (*Payne v Cave* (1789)).
4. To be valid, a revocation of an offer must be communicated
   to the offeree. It would also be unfair for a legitimate offeree
   to lose the chance to enter a contract because the offer was
   withdrawn without warning (*Byrne v Van Tienhoven* (1880)).
5. The revocation need not be made personally. It can be made by
   a reliable third party, i.e. one known to both parties so that the
   offeree may rely on the revocation (*Dickinson v Dodds* (1876)).
6. A unilateral offer cannot be withdrawn if the offeree is in the
   act of performing, since acceptance and performance are one
   and the same thing (*Errington v Errington and Woods* (1952)).

2.2.4 Termination of offers

1. An offer may come to an end because it has been accepted, in which case a contract is formed.
2. Other than this an offer can end in one of three ways.
   (a) By passage of time:
      (i) because the time set for acceptance has passed;
      (ii) because a 'reasonable time' has passed – it would be unfair to expect an offeror to indefinitely keep open an offer for sale of perishable goods. What is a 'reasonable time' is thus a question of fact in each case (*Ramsgate Victoria Hotel v Montefiore* (1866)).
   (b) By failing to comply with a condition precedent (*Financings v Stimson* (1962)), e.g. an offer of employment made subject to production of a satisfactory reference or medical report.
   (c) Because of the death of either party.
      (i) If the offeror dies and the offeree knows of this, it is unlikely that (s)he would be able to accept and bind the estate of the offeror to a contract.
      (ii) If the offeree, however, accepts an offer in ignorance of the death of the offeror then a contract may be formed (*Bradbury v Morgan* (1862)).
      (iii) If the offeree dies then it is unlikely that the executors or administrators of the estate can accept on his/her behalf (*Reynolds v Atherton* (1921)).

2.3 ACCEPTANCE

2.3.1 The role of acceptance in agreement

1. A contract is not formed until an offer is accepted.
2. An agreement occurs when a 'valid' acceptance follows a 'valid' offer, and the contract is formed immediately on acceptance.
3. It is vital to establish that the response to the offer is in fact an acceptance and is properly communicated to the offeror.

4. However, not all negotiations are easily identifiable as offer and acceptance, particularly negotiations in a commercial context.

The mirror image rule
- Acceptance must be unequivocal and unconditional – so must 'mirror' the offer in every way.
- An attempt to vary the terms of the offer is a counter offer, so the offer is no longer open to acceptance (*Hyde v Wrench*).
- A mere enquiry will not extinguish the offer (*Stevenson v McLean*).
- If an agreement continues after a counter offer is made the contract is based on the terms of the counter offer (*Davies & Co. v William Old*).

ACCEPTANCE

Communicating the acceptance
- Only a genuine offeree can accept an offer (*Powell v Lee*).
- Acceptance must be communicated to be valid.
- So silence can never be acceptance (*Felthouse v Bindley*).
- If a specific form of acceptance is required it must be in that form (*Compagnie de Commerce et Commissions S.A.R.L. v Parkinson Stove Co.*).
- There is no need to communicate acceptance of a unilateral offer (*Carlill v Carbolic Smoke Ball Co.*).
- If the post is the anticipated method of acceptance then acceptance occurs on posting of the letter (*Adams v Lindsell*).
- Acceptance applies even if letter is never received (*Household Fire Insurance Co. v Grant*).
- Modern methods of communication may be different (*Brinkibon v Stahag Stahl*).

The 'battle of the forms'
- Rules are difficult to apply to standard form contracts.
- So judges struggle to find an agreement (*British Steel Corporation v Cleveland Bridge Engineering Co*).
- One answer is to replace the contested terms by implying reasonable ones (*Butler Machine Tool Co. Ltd. v ExCell-O Corporation*).

2.3.2 The basic rules of acceptance

1. A valid acceptance is an intention to be bound by the terms of the offer, so it must:
   - be unequivocal and unconditional; and
   - correspond exactly with the terms of the offer – the 'mirror image' rule.
2. An attempt to vary the terms of the offer is a counter offer, which is a rejection of the offer that is no longer open to acceptance (*Hyde v Wrench* (1840)).
3. A rejection of an ancillary subject may still be a counter offer, although the main terms are accepted (*Jones v Daniel* (1894)).
4. However, a mere enquiry that does not seek to vary the terms of the offer is not a counter offer (*Stevenson v McLean* (1880)).
5. If arrangements continue after a counter offer is made then it is the terms of the counter offer that are included in the contract (*Davies & Co. v William Old* (1969)).
6. But the courts will not allow a party to benefit from both the counter offer and the original offer (*Pars Technology v City Link Transport Holdings Ltd* (1999)).
7. This may not result if the parties are not interested in ancillary terms and have overlooked the discrepancy in terms (*Brogden v Metropolitan Railway Co.* (1877)).

2.3.3 The 'battle of the forms'

1. Basing the contract on the counter offer causes problems in commercial contracts based on parties' 'standard forms'.
2. Parties may eventually contract after protracted negotiations, but it is the final set of terms that are taken as binding on the parties.
3. The courts may decide that there is no valid offer and acceptance and halt performance.
4. However, the courts are reluctant to do so once performance has begun (*British Steel Corp. v Cleveland Bridge & Engineering Co.* (1984)).
5. In *Butler Machine Tool Co. Ltd v Ex-Cell-O Corp.* (1979) Lord Denning suggested that 'If differences are irreconcilable, so

that they are mutually contradictory, then the conflicting terms may have to be scrapped and replaced by a reasonable implication.' However, most judges would not follow this.

6. Lord Lloyd has suggested that a contract can run with the vital terms agreed and some ancillary terms still to be agreed (*Pagnan SpA v Feed Products Ltd.* (1987)).

2.3.4 Communication of the acceptance

1. There is no contract unless acceptance is communicated.

2. Only a genuine offeree can accept the offer, so an offer made without authority cannot be accepted (*Powell v Lee* (1908)).

3. It follows that silence cannot amount to an acceptance (*Felthouse v Bindley* (1863)).

4. In some situations communication can be waived, e.g. unilateral contracts or customary conduct between parties.

5. Generally, acceptance can be in any form, but if a specific method of acceptance is known to be required then acceptance must be in that form to be valid (*Compagnie de Commerce et Commissions S.A.R.L. v Parkinson Stove Co.* (1953)).

6. Acceptance of a unilateral offer need not be communicated, because performance is the same as acceptance (*Carlill v Carbolic Smoke Ball Co.* (1893)).

7. In one situation the acceptance takes place before the offeror receives notification of it – this is the 'postal rule'.

(a) Where use of the post is the normal, anticipated method of acceptance, the acceptance is valid and the contract formed when the letter is posted, not when it is received by the offeror (*Adams v Lindsell* (1818)).

(b) The rule applies where the letter of acceptance is received after notice of revocation of the offer is sent (*Henthorn v Fraser* (1892)).

(c) It can also apply even though the letter of acceptance is never received (*Household Fire Insurance Co. v Grant* (1879)).

(d) The postal rule can be excluded by the terms of the offer itself (*Holwell Securities v Hughes* (1974)).

8. The postal rule has limited application to modern communications technology. In *Entores Ltd. v Miles Far East Corp.* (1955), offer and acceptance communicated by telex were valid because the method was so instantaneous that the parties were deemed to be dealing as if face to face, even though they were in different countries.

● The reason is that such forms of communication are usually instantaneous (*Brinkibon v Stahag Stahl* (1983)).
● The time when these forms of communication are used may cause problems in determining if a contract is made, as when a fax is sent out of office hours.

9. Now offer and acceptance in the case of electronic communication is governed by the Consumer Protection (Distance Selling) Regulations 2000. This gives the buyer the right to be informed of right to cancel within seven days, description, price, arrangements for payment and identity of seller, and to be given written confirmation, without which contract is not formed. Under EU Electronic Commerce Directive 2000/31, no contract can be made electronically until the buyer has received acknowledgement of his acceptance.

2.4 CONSIDERATION

2.4.1 The nature and purpose of consideration

1. Contract law concerns enforcement of promises based on mutual agreement.
2. In the early forms of contract law (debt, detinue, covenant) proof that a binding agreement existed was easily found in the form of the agreement, i.e. was only binding if under seal.
3. Enforcing informal agreements developed in the sixteenth century with the law of assumpsit:

● the law would still not enforce merely gratuitous promises,

Definitions
- Benefit/detriment (*Currie v Misa*).
- The promise of the one is the price for which the promise of the other is bought (*Dunlop v Selfridge*).

Consideration need not be adequate
- It need not equal the value of the other thing (*Thomas v Thomas*).

Must be sufficient
- It must be real (*White v Bluett*).
- It must be tangible (*Chappel v Nestle*).
- It must be of value (*Ward v Byham*).
- However, what is sufficient can in fact be very little.

CONSIDERATION

Considerations must not be past
- The consideration should not come before any agreement (*Re McArdle*),
- unless the service was requested – the rule in (*Lampleigh v Braithwaite*).

Consideration must move from the promissee:
To sue or be sued a party must give consideration (*Tweddle v Atkinson*)

Part payment of a debt
- an agreement to accept part payment only is unenforceable (*Pinnel's rule*),
- unless the payment is made earlier or in different form (*D C Builders v Rees*),
- or the other party is prevented from revoking the promise through estoppel (*Central London Properties Trust v High Trees House*).

Existing contractual or public duties
- What one is bound to do under an existing contract cannot be consideration for a fresh promise (*Stilk v Myrick*),
- unless it involves something extra (*Hartley v Ponsonby*)
- or unless the other party gains an extra benefit (*Williams v Roffey Brothers & Nicholls Contractors*).

- so the law had to develop an element that could distinguish between a proper contractual agreement which would be enforced, and something less that would not.

4. This was the origin of the element of consideration.

   (a) Proof was required that the party seeking to enforce the contract was in fact a party to a mutual agreement by contributing something in return for the promise of the other party.
   (b) This was the *quid pro quo* – one thing in return for another.
   (c) In the sixteenth and seventeenth centuries the courts asked for evidence of the existence of this extra element before they would acknowledge the existence of the agreement in law.
   (d) Defining consideration was and remains a problem.

2.4.2 Defining consideration

1. Originally no single definition could be found.
2. Often the view taken was that consideration was no more than the reason why the promise should be enforced in the case.
3. It was first seen as a rule of evidence, and later as a moral obligation, neither of which makes consideration an essential in identifying a binding contract.
4. Nineteenth-century judges saw the essential difference between speciality agreements and 'parol' agreements (*Eastwood v Kenyon* (1840)).
5. So nineteenth-century judges defined consideration in terms of benefit gained and detriment suffered:

   - 'loss or convenience sustained by one party at the request of another' (*Bunn v Guy* (1803));
   - 'some detriment to the plaintiff or some benefit to the defendant' (*Thomas v Thomas* (1842));
   - 'some right, interest, profit or benefit accruing to one party, or some forbearance, detriment, loss or responsibility given, suffered or undertaken by the other' (*Currie v Misa* (1875)).

6. The benefit/detriment relationship has obvious problems.

- Most modern agreements are executory, and so at the time of the promise neither party is actually suffering a detriment.
- Promises to give up something harmful in return for a price may be a detriment even though an advantage is gained.
- In a good bargain paying for goods or services of higher value can hardly be seen as a detriment or loss.

7. So the more modern definition in *Dunlop v Selfridge* (1915) is to do with exchange.

(a) It repeats Sir Frederick Pollock's definition in *Principles of Contract*: 'An act of forbearance of one party, or the promise thereof, is the price for which the promise of the other is bought, and the promise thus given for value is enforceable'.

(b) This definition is still problematic, i.e. if a judge construes consideration to enforce an agreement induced by actions of one party, or because of the context of the promise (*Williams v Roffey Bros. & Nicholls Contractors* (1990)).

2.4.3 Executed and executory consideration

1. The definition means both promises and acts are enforceable.

2. Executory consideration is where a promise to perform under the contract is given in return for a similar promise by the other party, e.g. goods ordered in return for a promise to pay the set price.

3. Executed consideration is consideration that is already given, e.g. money claimed under a reward.

4. So the difference between the two is often seen as the difference between bilateral and unilateral agreements.

2.4.4 Rules of consideration

Consideration need not be adequate

1. The law of contract regulates the making of bargains.
2. As freedom of contract is vital the law is not concerned with whether a party has made a good bargain or a bad one.
3. Adequacy is given its normal meaning – the contract is enforceable even if the price does not match the value of what is being gained under the agreement (*Thomas v Thomas* (1842)).

Consideration must be sufficient

1. In this context sufficiency is given a precise legal meaning.
2. Consideration offered is therefore 'sufficient' provided that:
   - it is real (*White v Bluett* (1853));
   - it is tangible (*Ward v Byham* (1956));
   - it has some discernible value (*Chappel v Nestle* (1960)). And economic value is measured against benefit gained (*Edmonds v Lawson* (2000)) on payment of trainee barristers during pupillage.
3. It is arguable that judges find consideration exists whenever they wish to enforce a particular agreement, regardless of the difficulties involved (*Alliance Bank v Broom* (1864)).
4. This may lead to an apparent contradiction with the other basic rules (*Williams v Roffey Bros. & Nicholls* (1990)).

Consideration must not be past

1. Consideration must follow rather than precede agreement.
   (a) This prevents coercion by suppliers of goods or services.
   (b) The rule acts in a similar manner to the Unsolicited Goods and Services Act 1971.
2. If a party carries out a voluntary act with no mention of payment at the time, then the law concludes that no payment is expected.

(a) Since the act is gratuitous any later promise to pay for the service by the other party, therefore, is unenforceable, however harsh this may seem (*Re McArdle* (1951)).

b) An agreement reached after consideration has passed is not an agreement, since it could not have been based on a mutual position (*Roscorla v Thomas* (1842)).

3. An exception is the rule in *Lampleigh v Braithwaite* (1615).

(a) This applies where the service was originally requested by one party and is then carried out by the other party.

(b) A later promise to pay is enforceable, even though the agreement to pay comes after the service is rendered (or, in other words, consideration is provided).

(c) Reason for the rule is that requesting service implies that there should have been original willingness to pay.

4. Both rule and exception can be shown in diagram form:

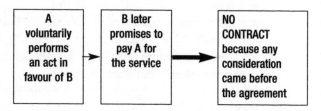

Past consideration in action

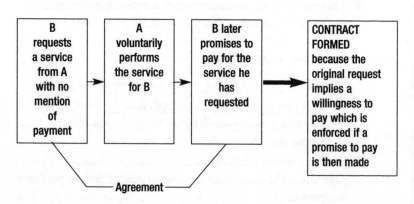

The exception in *Lampleigh v Braithwaite* in action

Consideration must move from the promissee

1. This rule goes hand-in-hand with the doctrine of privity.
2. The rule is that only a person who has provided consideration under a contract can sue or be sued under the contract.
3. So third parties who appear to have rights under the contract are nevertheless denied an action (*Tweddle v Atkinson* (1861)).
4. An exception is where third parties seek to enforce collateral warranties on which they have relied (*Shanklin Pier Ltd. v Detel Products Ltd.* (1951)).
5. The rule will also not now apply where it is affected by the Contracts (Rights of Third Parties) Act 1999.
6. The Act applies if third parties are identified in the contract as having the right to enforce it, or in circumstances where a third party is shown to have gained rights under the contract.

New agreements and performance of existing obligations

1. A person can never use performing something (s)he is already bound to do under an existing contract as consideration for a new agreement (*Stilk v Myrick* (1809)).
2. This also applies for public duties which, if carried out, cannot be consideration for a new contractual arrangement (*Collins v Godefroy* (1831)).
3. However, there are exceptions to the basic rule.
   (a) If something extra is given above that required under the original contract then there is consideration for new agreement (*Hartley v Ponsonby* (1857)).
   (b) If something more than the basic public or legal duty is added that is also consideration for the new agreement (*Glasbrook Bros. v Glamorgan County Council* (1925)).
   (c) If third parties' rights are affected by the performance of the existing contract (*Pao On v Lao Yiu Long* (1980)) this is consideration.
   (d) If the integrity of a commercial arrangement is preserved by performance of existing contractual obligations (*New Zealand Shipping Co. Ltd. v A.M. Satterthwaite & Co. Ltd. (The Eurymedon)* (1975)) this is consideration.

(e) More recently, if a party promising to accept performance of an existing contractual obligation as consideration for a new agreement gains an extra benefit from that performance this can be consideration for the new agreement (*Williams v Roffey Bros. & Nicholls (Contractors) Ltd.* (1990)).

Part-payment of debts

1. The basic rule in *Pinnel's case* (1602) is that part-payment of a debt can never satisfy the whole debt.

2. Any agreement to accept part-payment in full satisfaction of the debt is unenforceable, as it lacks consideration.

3. The rule operates fairly when the debtor is trying to avoid the debt by extracting the promise (*D C Builders v Rees* (1965)).

4. The rule can also act unfairly where the creditor goes back on a promise made on which the debtor has relied in determining his future course of conduct (*Foakes v Beer* (1884)).

5. As a result the courts have developed exceptions to the rule.

6. The first exception is where something different is added to the part-payment, or the payment is made in another form – since a waiver of rights must be supported by consideration.

   (a) This was identified in *Pinnel's case* itself.

   (b) The court accepts part-payment because the new element in fact represents consideration for the new agreement, e.g.:

   - an agreement to accept a smaller sum at an earlier date;
   - or to accept payment in a form other than money;
   - or to accept a lesser sum of money together with something other than money.

7. The second exception is the doctrine of promissory estoppel.

   (a) This was first recognised by Lord Cairns in *Hughes v Metropolitan Railway Co.* (1877) as being based on the doctrine of waiver – that a party should be prevented from going back on a promise to waive rights (though the case concerned waiver in the context of property rights).

(b)   Lord Denning reintroduced and developed it in contract law in *Central London Properties Trust Co. Ltd. v High Trees House Ltd.* (1947), stating that: 'if one party promises to forego or not to rely upon his strict legal rights and the other party, in reliance on that promise, acts upon it, then the promisor is estopped from asserting his full legal rights'.

(c)   This caused confusion, so Lord Denning explained four key ingredients of the principle in *Coombe v Coombe* (1951):

- there must be a pre-existing contractual relationship;
- one party within that contractual relationship agrees to waive rights (s)he is entitled to under that agreement;
- and does so knowing that the other party relies on the waiver in determining their future course of conduct;
- the other party does actually rely on the waiver.

(d)   If all of these are present then the party agreeing to waive contractual rights is prevented by equity (estopped) from going back on the agreement to waive the rights.

(e)   However, in *Coombe v Coombe* it was said that estoppel is 'a shield and not a sword', so it is a defence against a person who is going back on a promise to waive rights under the contract, but not a means of bringing an action.

(f)   The doctrine is equitable so is at the discretion of the court.

(g)   Many later attempts to develop the principle have been rejected (*Brikom Investments Ltd. v Carr* (1979)).

8. A more recent attempt to apply the principles found in *Williams v Roffey Bros. & Nicholls (Contractors) Ltd.* (1990) to cover agreements to accept part payment of a debt in full satisfaction has also been rejected in *Re Selectmove Ltd.* (1995).

INTENTION TO CREATE LEGAL RELATIONS

Based on two rebuttable presumptions

Domestic and social arrangements

There is presumed to be no intention to create legal relations unless the contrary is shown

Agreements not usually enforceable:
- husband and wife (*Balfour v Balfour*);
- parents and children (*Jones v Padavatton*).

Agreements usually enforceable:
- estranged couples (*Merritt v Merritt*);
- domestic agreements where money has changed hands (*Simpkins v Pays*);
- domestic arrangements where one party has suffered a detriment to comply with the agreement (*Parker v Clark*).

Business and commercial transactions

There is presumed to be an intention to create legal relations unless the contrary is shown

Agreements usually enforceable:
- Informal arrangements linked to a legal requirement (*Edwards v Skyways*);
- free gifts made to increase business (*Esso Petroleum v Commissioners of Customs & Excise*).

Agreements not usually enforceable:
- specifically written to exclude legal enforcement (*Jones v Vernons Pools*);
- honour pledge clauses (*Rose and Frank v Crompton Bros.*);
- comfort letters (*Kleinwort Benson Ltd. v Malaysia Mining Corporation*).

2.5 INTENTION TO CREATE LEGAL RELATIONS

2.5.1 The character and purpose of the rule

1. The rule has a clear purpose – to prevent the courts being clogged up with disputes to which no legal liability should be attached.
2. Lord Stowell in *Dalrymple v Dalrymple* (1811) said contracts should not be 'the sports of an idle hour, mere matters of pleasantry and badinage, never intended by the parties to have any serious effect whatever'.
3. So the law distinguishes between agreements needing the support of law and enforceable in the courts, and entirely gratuitous promises where the law should not intervene.
4. Determining which agreements are enforceable or not developed through case law using two rebuttable presumptions:

   * if agreements are purely domestic or social in nature the presumption is that there is no intention that the agreement should be legally enforceable;
   * in a business or commercial context the presumption is that the parties do intend agreements to be legally binding.
5. In either case the individuals in the dispute might challenge the presumption with evidence to the contrary.

2.5.2 Social and domestic arrangements

1. Agreements between husbands and wives will not usually create legal relations as the courts are unwilling to interfere in the internal relations of a marriage (*Balfour v Balfour* (1919).
2. This is different if the couple were estranged before the agreement was reached (*Merritt v Merritt* (1970)).
3. Arrangements between parents and children do not usually create a legal relationship, especially if the agreement is seen as vague or ambiguous (*Jones v Padavatton* (1969)).

4. The presumption is rebutted if a party suffers an obvious detriment because of a domestic agreement and the agreement is then enforceable (*Parker v Clark* (1960)).

5. If money is given under the agreement it is more likely to be seen as intended to be legally enforceable despite the social or domestic context (*Simpkins v Pays* (1955)).

6. The courts can accept that the agreement is severable with some parts legally enforceable and others not (*Julian v Furby* (1982)).

2.5.3 Commercial and business dealings

1. An informal agreement made in a broader business context may still be legally enforceable (*Edwards v Skyways Ltd.* (1964)).

2. Giving free gifts may create legally enforceable arrangements if actually a disguised way of extending business (*Esso Petroleum Ltd. v Commissioners of Customs and Excise* (1976)), as will prizes given in competitions (*McGowan v Radio Buxton* (2001)).

3. It is, however, possible to expressly exclude the possibility of legal enforceability within the agreement itself, as when the arrangement is of a kind not normally recognised as enforceable in contract law (*Jones v Vernons Pools* (1938)).

4. So-called 'honour pledge clauses', binding in honour but not law, have also failed to create legal relations between parties (*Rose and Frank Co. v J R Crompton & Brothers Ltd.* (1925)).

5. Mere 'comfort letters' showing a willingness to guarantee the debts of subsidiary companies have also failed (*Kleinwort Benson Ltd. v Malaysia Mining Corporation Bhd* (1989)).

6. Comfort letters on the proposed sale and purchase of a company have also been held as unenforceable (*Walford v Miles* (1992)).

7. For policy reasons so have informal arrangements entered into by public bodies, e.g. paying informers (*Robinson v Customs and Excise Commissioners* (2000)).

CHAPTER 3

OTHER FACTORS AFFECTING FORMATION

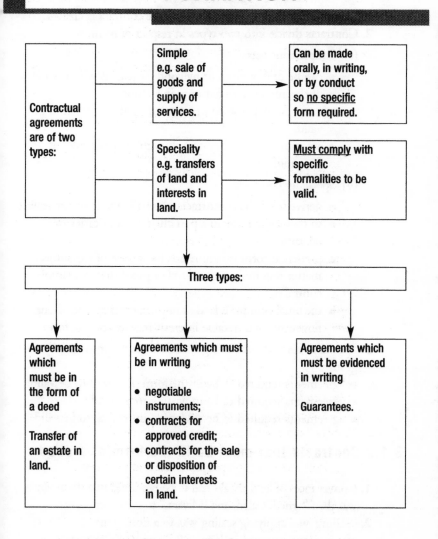

The importance of form in contracts

3.1 FORM

3.1.1 The character of contracts

1. Form refers to the manner in which the contract is created.

2. Contracts divide into two types in respect of form.

(a) Simple contracts:

- can be oral, written or by conduct (e.g. as with the fall of the auctioneer's hammer in auctions);
- come from 'parol' contracts – no particular form to be valid;
- are enforceable if they comply with the basic rules of formation.

(b) Speciality contracts:

- derive from those contracts originally made under seal;
- so they need to be in a particular form in order to be valid;
- particular form is required as the nature of the subject matter requires a higher level of proof than for simple contracts;
- the usual example is land or other interests in land, though now other transferable interests require specific form

3. Speciality contracts requiring specific form fall into three groups:

- agreements required to be in the form of a deed to be valid;
- agreements required to be in writing to be valid;
- agreements required to be evidenced in writing to be valid.

3.1.2 Contracts that must be in the form of a deed

1. Conveyances of land always had to be produced in a deed which was then 'signed, sealed, and delivered' to the other party.

2. 'Sealing' was applying sealing wax to a document, a requirement removed in Law of Property (Miscellaneous Provisions) Act 1989.

3. Now, by s1(2) of the 1989 Act for a deed to be valid it must:

   (a) be clear on its face that it is intended to act as a deed; and
   (b) be validly executed.

4. By s1(3) of the 1989 Act it will be validly executed if it is signed, the signature is witnessed, and it is delivered as a deed.

5. A deed is one method of ensuring that entirely gratuitous arrangements such as charitable gifts are legally enforceable.

3.1.3   Contracts that must be in writing to be valid

1. Contracts required to be in writing are usually identified in statute.
2. Written form is the means of establishing authenticity.
3. Contracts involving negotiable instruments (e.g. cheques).

   * These were originally authorised by the Bills of Exchange Act 1882, but are also governed by subsequent Acts.
   * If the instrument is in writing then it will be valid.
   * Rules of signing, endorsing, crossing etc. also apply.

4. Contracts of approved credit:

   * These are governed by the Consumer Credit Act 1974.
   * There are other requirements besides written form.

5. Contracts for sale or other disposition of an interest in land.

   * Formerly regulated by s40 Law of Property Act 1925.
   * Such contracts were required to be in writing unless the doctrine of part-performance applied.
   * The Law of Property (Miscellaneous Provisions) Act 1989 has repealed both s40 and the doctrine of part-performance.
   * Now such contracts must:
     (a) be in writing; and
     (b) incorporate all of the terms agreed by the parties; and
     (c) be signed by or on behalf of each party.
   * Repeal of the doctrine of part-performance makes it more difficult for equity to intervene in a dispute over lack of form.

3.1.4 Contracts needing evidence in writing to be valid

1. These were formerly governed by the Statute of Frauds 1677.
2. With the repeal of s40 Law of Property Act 1925 the only contract falling within this category is a contract of guarantee.
3. A contract of guarantee is a promise by one party made to a second party in respect of a debt owed to the second party by a third party – agreeing to stand those debts in the event of default by the third-party debtor.
4. Under s4 Statute of Frauds 1677 a guarantee must be evidenced in writing, which need only be a note or memorandum, and:

   - the memorandum does not need to be in a particular form;
   - it must be signed by the guarantor or his/her agent;
   - and an admission of the existence of the contract of guarantee;
   - so must contain all material terms of the guarantee, including the identity of parties and subject matter of the agreement.

5. A guarantee should be distinguished from an indemnity.

   - A guarantor 'stands in the shoes of the principal debtor', the guarantee is only enforceable if evidenced in writing.
   - An indemnity is an agreement to take on the debts of the debtor and therefore is not covered by the 1677 Act.

Drunkenness and capacity

- A contract made by a person while drunk is voidable if:
  a) at the time of contracting the person did not know the quality of his/her acts (*Gore v Gibson*);
  b) the other party knew of the intoxication.
- The party may ratify the contract on becoming sober (*Matthews v Baxter*).
- By s3 Sale of Goods Act 1979, where the contract is for necessaries, the party making the contract while drunk need only pay a reasonable price for goods actually delivered.

Mental illness and capacity

- It would obviously be unjust to take advantage of someone's mental illness, so a contract made while someone is mentally ill is voidable if:
  a) when contracting the mentally ill person was unaware of the quality of his/her actions (*Imperial Loan Co. v Stone*);
  b) the other party knew of the illness.
- A contract made while not ill will be binding even if the person then becomes ill again.
- By s3 Sale of Goods Act 1979, in a contract for necessaries the party is only bound to pay a reasonable price for goods actually delivered.

CAPACITY

Corporations and capacity

- A corporation has a separate legal personality and can sue and be sued in its own name.
- Corporations are created in one of three ways, the manner of creation determining the capacity:
  a) by Royal Charter, e.g. the original trading companies, such as the East Indies Co. – the capacity is limited by whatever is in the charter;
  b) by statute – the capacity is spelt out in the Act itself;
  c) by registration under the Companies Acts – the powers of the company to act are in the objects clause in the memorandum of association.
- Traditionally the *ultra vires doctrine* meant that a company could not act beyond its powers (*Ashbury Railway Carriage Co. Ltd. v Richie*).
- Nor can a company use an ancillary power for improper purposes (*Introductions Ltd. v National Provincial Bank Ltd.*).
- Now governed by s35 Companies Act 1985 as amended by s108 Companies Act 1989:
  a) a transaction made by the directors is deemed to be one of that can be made;
  b) third parties can enforce such agreements and have them enforced against them;
  c) shareholders can use injunctions to prevent directors from entering *ultra vires* transactions.

3.2 CAPACITY

3.2.1 The nature and purpose of capacity

1. Better described as incapacity as it concerns limits on a party's capacity to contract, or limitations imposed on the other party.
2. Every person is assumed to have capacity to enter a contract, though certain groups are identified as lacking full capacity. This is to protect freedom of contract, so where a person lacks capacity it is to protect him/her from being taken advantage of.
3. Rules exist for three distinct groups of natural persons.

    (a) Minors – people under the age of 18.

      - This is the most important group.
      - Some contracts are enforceable against them, some are unenforceable, some can be made by the minor but avoided before age 18 or a reasonable time.

    (b) Drunkards – where a person is so intoxicated as to be unaware of the quality of agreements made while drunk.

    (c) People suffering mental incapacity – either temporary or permanent, but the person is presumed to be unaware of the quality of any agreement made while mentally ill.

4. Rules on capacity also cover non-natural persons – corporations with a separate legal personality, which can sue or be sued in their own name.

3.2.2 Drunkenness and capacity

1. A party who enters a contract while drunk may consider the contract unenforceable against him in certain circumstances:

    - the party must not have known the quality of his/her actions at the time the contract was formed (*Gore v Gibson* (1845));
    - the other party must have known of the intoxication.

2. The contract is voidable when the drunken party is sober.
3. A party may ratify an agreement on becoming sober (*Matthews v Baxter* (1873)).
4. By s3 Sale of Goods Act 1979, even if the contract is enforceable, e.g. necessaries, if incapacitated by drink need only pay a reasonable price for goods delivered.

3.2.3 Mentally disordered people and capacity

1. Understanding of mental illness increased in the last century.
2. Numerous statutory rules have developed for the administration of the property of such people.
3. Common law still mainly controls their contractual capacity.
4. The court must first decide if, when the contract was formed, the person was incapable of understanding the quality of their act.

   - So the contract is voidable by person lacking mental capacity (*Imperial Loan Co. v Stone* (1892)).
   - The other party must have known of the mental incapacity.

5. Contract made in a period of lucidity is binding on the mentally incapacitated person even if (s)he becomes sick again.
6. By s3 Sale of Goods Act 1979, in a contract for necessaries the person need only pay a reasonable price for goods already supplied, even if the other party is unaware of the mental illness.

3.2.4 Corporations and capacity

1. Corporations should not be confused with unincorporated associations, e.g. clubs, where members are jointly or severally liable for contracts, and the club can neither sue or be sued.
2. A corporation has a separate legal personality, but not being a natural person has limitations on its capacity determined by its method of creation.

3. A corporation will be formed in one of three ways:

- by Royal Charter, e.g. the original trading companies, such as the East India Company – the capacity to contract will be dictated by the terms of the charter, and is usually wide;
- by statute, e.g. the nationalised industries which later became privatised – the capacity of the corporation is dictated by the wording of the statute creating it;
- by registration under the Companies Acts – the capacity of the company is identified in the constitution found in the Memorandum of Association in the 'objects clause'.

4. Traditionally a company's contractual capacity was regulated by the *ultra vires* doctrine, i.e. it could not act beyond its powers and act for purposes not identified in the objects clause (*Ashbury Railway Carriage Co. Ltd. v Richie* (1875)).

5. The *ultra vires* doctrine is also applied to using ancillary power for improper purposes (*Introductions Ltd. v National Provincial Bank Ltd* (1970)).

6. Originally companies could plead their own *ultra vires* to defeat claims of parties contracting with them, since people were fixed with constructive notice of the objects clause.

7. S35 Companies Act 1985 overcame this by stating that where a party deals with company in good faith, 'any transaction decided on by the directors shall be deemed to be one which is within the capacity of the company to enter into, and the power of the directors to bind the company shall be deemed to be free of any limitations in the memorandum'.

8. S35 has now also been amended by s108 Companies Act 1989 which operates in three ways.

(a) It provides that an act is not invalidated merely because it is beyond the company's capacity:

- so third parties can enforce agreements with the company;
- the company can enforce agreements against the third party;
- shareholders may use injunctions to prevent *ultra vires* actions;

● construction of the objects clause is wider so it can be drafted in wider terms than previously.

(b) A new s35A means a third party's knowledge of directors acting beyond their powers is not of itself bad faith.

(c) A new s35B removes the need to inquire whether or not the transaction is one allowed by the objects clause.

3.3 CAPACITY AND MINORS' CONTRACTS

3.3.1 The basic principle of minority

1. The modern definition of minority is in the Family Law Reform Act 1969.

2. Under the Act the previous use of the word 'infant' was abandoned and the age of majority reduced from 21 to 18.

3. The Act possibly reduced the significance of the area for a while by taking many people out of the scope of the rules.

4. With the increased independence of young people this effect may have reduced.

3.3.2 The character and purpose of rules

1. As minors are less experienced the law decides that they need protection from adults who would take advantage of them.

2. They are not prevented from making contracts, but the consequences for the other party to the contract may vary.

3. Minors' contracts fall into three basic categories.

● Valid contracts – those enforceable against the minor.

● Voidable contracts – those the minor may enter and possibly continue with, but also avoid or set aside.

● Void contracts – those that can never be enforced against the minor, so other parties will be reluctant to make them.

Valid and enforceable against the minor

Necessaries:

- must pay reasonable price for goods or services actually delivered (*Chapple v Cooper & s3SGA*, (1979);
- Necessary means:
  a) according to station in life,
  b) and present needs (*Nash v Inman*).

Education, training, service substantially to minor's benefit:

- one adverse term will not invalidate the contract (*Clements v LNWR*);
- but must be substantially to minor's benefit (*De Francesco v Barnum*).

Voidable by the minor

- Known as contracts of 'continuous or recurrent obligation'.
- Minor can continue with contract or avoid it by 18 or reasonable time thereafter.
- There are four types:
  a) contracts to lease property;
  b) contracts to purchase shares in a company;
  c) contracts to join a partnership;
  d) marriage settlements.
- Question of fact in each case whether the minor has repudiated in time (*Edwards v Carter*).
- If minor repudiates before obligations arise (s)he is not bound by ones arising later.
- Money already transferred by the minor is only recoverable if a failure of consideration (*Steinberg v Scala (Leeds) Ltd.*).
- However, it may be recoverable if (s)he has not received what was promised under the agreement (*Corpe v Overton*).

MINORS' CONTRACTS

Role of equity

- Equity formerly allowed recovery of property to prevent a minor's 'unjust enrichment' (*Leslie v Sheill*).
- Now s3 Minor's Contract Act allows recovery where it is 'just and equitable'.

Void and unenforceable against the minor

- Anything not valid or voidable is void and unenforceable against the minor
- Includes:
  a) loans;
  b) goods or services other than necessaries;
  c) accounts stated (IOUs).
- May still be enforceable against the other party.
- Property may be recovered by minor if an absence of consideration.
- Now in s2 Minors' Contract Act guarantees are enforceable to allow minors to make loans.

3.3.3 Contracts valid and enforceable against minors

1. These contain two distinct groups:

  * contracts for necessaries;
  * contracts of service, training or education substantially for the benefit of the minor.

2. Contracts for necessaries.

  (a) Common law demands that a minor pays a reasonable price for necessaries actually delivered (*Chapple v Cooper* (1844)).

  (b) Necessary is clearly variable – as well as food and clothing it must include what is necessary to the particular minor.

  (c) There is a two-part test in *Nash v Inman* (1908) – for a contract to be enforceable the goods or services must be:
      (i) necessary by the minor's 'station in life'; and
      (ii) necessary for the minor's actual current needs.

  (d) By s3 Sale of Goods Act 1979 a minor must only pay a reasonable price for goods actually delivered – which need not be the same as the agreed price.

  (e) Even if the contract is for necessaries the minor may not be bound by it if the contract terms are prejudicial to the minor's interests (*Fawcett v Smethurst* (1914)).

3. Beneficial contracts of service, training or education:

  (a) enforceable since the minor must be able to support himself, and school leaving age is 16, two years under majority;

  (b) nevertheless, the minor is given protection;

  (c) so contract is only enforceable if substantially for the minor's benefit;

  (d) the fact that some terms are detrimental will not automatically invalidate the contract (*Clements v London and North Western Railway Co.* (1894));

  (e) but if generally detrimental to the minor's interests the contract is not enforceable (*De Francesco v Barnum* (1890));

(f) contracts of service have included sporting contracts (*Doyle v White City Stadium Ltd.* (1935));

(g) and also contracts for literary works (*Chaplin v Leslie Frewin (Publishers) Ltd.* (1966));

(h) and since the minor needs to develop skills, as well as work, contracts for training, education and apprenticeship are also included (*Olsen v Corry* (1936));

(i) if the minor has entered such a contract which is declared to be not for his/her benefit then it is voidable by him/her.

3.3.4 Contracts voidable by minors

1. The common feature is that contracts can be long term, so known as contracts of continuous or recurring obligations.

2. The law concludes that, while minors should be able to enter such contracts they must also be allowed to back out of them before they reach majority, or within a reasonable time afterwards.

3. There are four types of contract included in this category:

● contracts to lease property;
● contracts to purchase shares in a company;
● contracts to enter a partnership;
● contracts of marriage settlement.

4. If the minor fails to repudiate and continues with the contract (s)he is bound by all the obligations arising under it.

5. Whether a minor has repudiated in time to avoid the contract is a question of fact in each case (*Edwards v Carter* (1893)).

6. If the minor repudiates before any obligations arise then the contract simply ceases at that point and the minor cannot be sued on any obligations arising at a later stage.

7. A minor may be bound by obligations arising before repudiation.

8. If the minor has transferred money under the agreement this is not recoverable unless there is a failure of consideration (*Steinberg v Scala (Leeds) Ltd.* (1923)).

9. However, money paid over by the minor may be recoverable if (s)he has not received what was promised under the agreement (*Corpe v Overton* (1833)).

3.3.5 Contracts void and unenforceable against minors

1. Law was previously regulated in the Infants Relief Act 1874.
2. Its defects led to the passing of the Minors' Contract Act 1987, which unusually restored the common law on the area, subject to some modifications.
3. The basic principle is that any contract not under the two categories already discussed is void and unenforceable.
4. This has a number of consequences.

   - A minor is less likely to be able to enter this final class of contracts, since prudent people will avoid making them.
   - While such contracts may not be enforceable against the minor they will be against the other party to the contract.
   - A minor can only recover money already paid over if there is a total failure of consideration on the other side.
   - If the minor ratifies the contract after reaching 18 then it binds him/her, although ratification need not be express, continuing with the contract counts as implied ratification.

5. Contracts coming under this class are those formerly identified in s1 Infants Relief Act 1874:

   - loans of money;
   - supply of goods or services other than necessaries;
   - accounts stated (IOUs).

6. Guarantees were originally unenforceable as, under the Infants Relief Act 1874, a guarantor 'stands in the shoes of the principal debtor' – if the contract was unenforceable against the minor the same applied to a guarantor.
7. Since minors may need loans in modern times s2 Minors' Contract Act 1987 allows enforcement of a guarantee, making loans more available to minors in need of them.

3.3.6 Equity and minors' contracts

1. The rules protect minors from exploitation or being taken advantage of.
2. Other parties may need protection from unscrupulous minors who would take unfair advantage of the rules.
3. A party trying to recover property from a minor in an unenforceable contract might traditionally use equity for restitution of the property to prevent the minor's 'unjust enrichment' (*R Leslie Ltd. v Sheill* (1914)).
4. Equity has been replaced by s3 Minors' Contract Act 1987 by which property can be returned to the party dealing with the minor if 'just and equitable' in the circumstances.
5. This remedies having to prove fraud on the minor's part.

3.4 THIRD PARTY RIGHTS AND PRIVITY OF CONTRACT

3.4.1 The basic rule and its effects

1. Lord Haldane defined the basic rule in its modern form in *Dunlop Pneumatic Tyre Co. Ltd. v Selfridge & Co. Ltd.* (1915): 'only a person who is a party to a contract can sue on it. Our law knows nothing of a *jus quaesitum tertio* (in) a contract'.
2. There are a number of consequences of the basic rule.
   - A person receiving goods as a gift cannot sue personally in respect of defects in the goods.
   - Purchasers of the goods may sue for the defect but recover nominal damages only, having suffered no loss personally.
   - Remedies such as specific performance may be unavailable.
   - The rule may mean that performance cannot be enforced even though it has been paid for (*Price v Easton* (1833)).

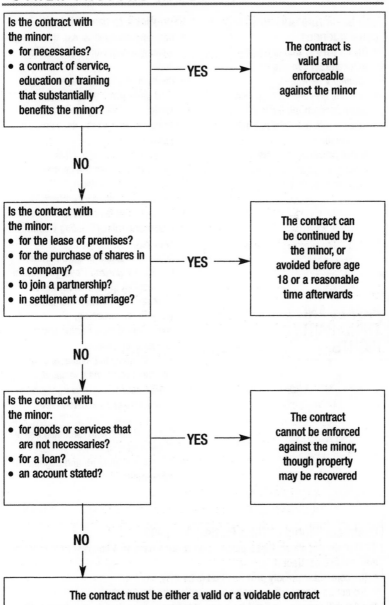

The effects of capacity on minors' contract

The basic rule and its consequences

- Only a person who is a party to a contract can sue on it (*Dunlop v Selfridge*).
- The rule prevents people also being sued on the basis of agreements that they are not a party to.
- It also prevents them from relying on rights that have been granted to them.

Exceptions to the strict rule

- Statutory exceptions, e.g. third party insurance under the Road Traffic Acts.
- Creation of a trust in favour of the third party (*Gregory & Parker v Williams*), providing the interest conforms with trust rules (*Green v Russell*).
- Restrictive covenants (*Tulk v Moxhay*), provided the contract is for land (*Taddy v Sterious*).
- The rule in *Dunlop v Lambert*.
- Privity of estates in leases.
- Procedural rules (*Snelling v John G Snelling*).
- Actions on behalf of third parties (*Jackson v Horizon Holidays*), but this only applies in the holiday cases (*Woodar Investment Development v Wimpey Construction*).
- Protection of third parties under exclusion clauses:
  a) traditionally not available to third parties (*Scruttons v Midland Silicones*);
  b) but have been allowed (*The Eurymedon*).
- Collateral contracts (*Shanklin Pier v Detel Products*).
- Agency, assignment, and negotiable instruments.

PRIVITY AND THIRD PARTY RIGHTS

Contracts (Rights of Third Parties) Act 1999

S1(1) of the Act allows that a person who is not a party to a contract (a third party) may enforce contract if:

- the contract expressly provides that (s)he may, or
- the contract purports to confer a benefit on the third party.

The Act will remove the need for many of the exceptions, but does not cover all contracts, e.g. employment contracts, bills of exchange, agency, insurance.

Parties in any case can exclude operation of the Act.

- The rule may have the effect of denying the express wishes of benefactors (*Tweddle v Atkinson* (1861)).
- A person could dishonour a commercial agreement (s)he has made in which another party has legitimate expectations (*Dunlop Pneumatic Tyre Co. v Selfridge & Co.* (1915)).

3.4.2 Problems with the privity rule

1. The doctrine of privity is probably the most contentious of all the rules of contract law.
2. The basic rule is that a person who is not a party to a contract can neither sue on it nor be sued under it.
3. Many justifications are made for the rule, but none is satisfactory.

   - It is linked to the doctrine of consideration, so that a person can neither sue on nor be sued under a contract that (s)he has not provided consideration for.
   - It is said to be unfair to impose obligations on a person who has not expressly entered a contractual agreement.
   - It is argued that it is unfair to allow a party to sue on a contract under which (s)he could not be sued.
   - It is not possible to sue in contract law for a purely gratuitous promise, which an agreement lacking privity on the part of one party could clearly be.

4. The rule operates unfairly in certain circumstances.

   - If a party is identified as gaining rights under a contract it is unfair not to allow that party to sue to enforce them.
   - If third party rights in an agreement are not enforceable then a primary purpose of the contract is being defeated.
   - If a third party suffers loss under a breach of an agreement between two other parties (s)he may get the innocent party to sue, but that party has suffered no loss so can only recover nominal damages, not an amount covering the breach.

5. So the rule has been heavily criticised, with two consequences:

   - the courts have been prepared to accept a number of different exceptions to the basic rule;

- Parliament has legislated for the protection of third party rights in certain circumstances.

3.4.3 Exceptions to the strict rule

1. Statutory exceptions.

(a) Parliament is not bound, so can legislate contrary to the rule.

(b) Examples of statutory exceptions include:

- S148(7) Road Traffic Act 1988 requires drivers to have third party insurance. This can then be relied upon by other road users they cause loss or injury to, despite lack of privity;
- S11 Married Woman's Property Act 1882 allowed a wife to claim on her husband's own life insurance policy;
- S14 Companies Act 1985, the 'statutory contract', allows shareholders to sue their companies on rights gained as a shareholder.

(c) However, using statute other than for its true purpose to avoid the privity rule has failed (*Beswick v Beswick* (1968)).

2. The law of trusts.

(a) Third parties have sued successfully (but in trust law not in contract law) by showing that the contract creates a trust of property in their favour (*Gregory & Parker v Williams* (1817)).

(b) Equity only intervenes if there is an express intention that the party claiming should receive the benefit (*Les Affreteurs Reunis SA v Walford* (1919)) *(Walford's case)*.

(c) Courts will only accept that a trust is created if the interest follows general trusts rules (*Green v Russell* (1959)).

3. Restrictive covenants.

(a) This is another equitable device whereby a person retains control to limit the use of land (s)he has sold, even against subsequent purchasers of the land.

(b) The restriction 'runs with the land' and binds each subsequent purchaser, even though they were not parties to the original agreement (*Tulk v Moxhay* (1848)).

(c) The device normally only operates in respect of land, so it could not apply to a price fixing agreement with tobacconists (*Taddy v Sterious* (1904) but see *Lord Strathcona Steamship Co. v Dominion Coal Co. Ltd.* (1926).

4. The rule in *Dunlop v Lambert* (1839).

(a) The rule stated that a remedy should be available despite the lack of privity where, 'no other would be available to a person sustaining loss which under a rational legal system ought to be compensated by the person who caused it'.

(b) It has limited application but was recently approved in an action by the assignee of the party in a contract who was a fiduciary of the third party (*Darlington B.C. v Wiltshier Northern Ltd.* (1995)). But see more restrictive approach in *Alfred McAlpine Construction v Panatown Ltd* (1998)).

5. Privity of estate in leases.

(a) Covenants in leases are enforceable between the original parties because they are also parties to the contract.

(b) Therefore the landlord can enforce such covenants against a party to whom the original tenant assigns the lease.

(c) By ss141 and 142 Law of Property Act 1925 a new tenant can enforce covenants against the landlord, and a new landlord can enforce covenants against existing tenants.

(d) A landlord cannot enforce covenants against a sub-tenant.

6. Procedural rules.

(a) Courts have accepted a rule of procedure in avoiding privity.

(b) However, they have only accepted it where to do so actually corresponds to the promise and because all of the parties are represented in the action (*Snelling v John G Snelling* (1973)).

7. Actions on behalf of a third party.

(a) The so-called 'holiday cases' allowed a contractor's family to also be represented in an award of damages despite their lack of privity (*Jackson v Horizon Holidays Ltd.* (1975)).

(b) However, the principle seems to be limited to holiday contracts (*Woodar Investment Development Ltd. v Wimpey Construction (UK) Ltd.* (1980)).

8. Rights of third parties to rely on exclusion clauses.

   (a) Traditionally a third party (e.g. a sub-contractor) could not rely on an exclusion clause even if the contract said that he could (*Scruttons Ltd. v Midland Silicones Ltd.* (1962)).

   (b) However, a different result was achieved where the third party was construed as having provided consideration even though not a party to the agreement (*New Zealand Shipping Co. Ltd. v A M Satterthwaite Co. Ltd.* (*The Eurymedon* (1975)).

9. Collateral contracts.

   (a) Where a third party makes a collateral warranty on which formation of the contract depends then a party to the contract may sue on the promise, even though it was not made by a party to the contract (*Shanklin Pier Ltd. v Detel Products Ltd.* (1951)).

   (b) The logic of the principle is based on the benefit being gained by the party making the collateral promise.

10. Agency, assignment, and negotiable instruments.

   (a) These are the major and the most common exceptions.

   (b) An agent represents a principal and so can bind the principal to contracts made with the third party and vice versa, and can sue or be sued for breaches of the agency agreement.

   (c) Assignment is a specific system of transferring rights in certain property – the assignee then owns the property and can sue or be sued by a party who had a contractual link to the property despite the apparent lack of privity.

   (d) Negotiable instruments were a device of merchant trading first given statutory effect in the Bills of Exchange Act 1882 – the commonest form today is the cheque. It can be transferred from party to party by endorsement, etc. and the new party gains all of the rights in the property of the former owner and can sue or be sued on the instrument.

3.4.4 Statutory intervention and the reform of the rule

1. General dissatisfaction with the rule is shown by judges' willingness to accept so many different exceptions to it.
2. Since it makes it impossible to exercise third party rights that are absolutely legitimate and intended by the contract.
3. Reform was demanded by judges and official reform bodies.
4. Law Commission Paper No. 121 concluded that there should be a 'third party rule' in privity, but with certain reservations:
   - it should not merely extend the exceptions to the rule;
   - it should not merely prevent the doctrine from interfering with any third party rights since this would be too vague;
   - it should make rights clearly intended in the contract itself to confer a benefit on the third party enforceable.
5. Law Commission Report No. 242 included a draft Bill, now enacted as the Contracts (Rights of Third Parties) Act 1999.
6. By s1(1): 'a person who is not a party to a contract (a third party) may in his own right enforce the contract if:
   (a) the contract expressly provides that he may, or
   (b) subject to subsection (2) the contract purports to confer a benefit on the third party'.
7. S1(2) states that 1(1)(b) is unavailable if, 'on the proper construction of the contract it appears that the parties did not intend the contract to be enforceable by the third party'.
8. By s1(3), the Act applies if the third party is identified in the contract by name or as a member of a class. The third party need not exist at the time the contract was formed.
9. Important exceptions where the Act will not apply include:
   - bills of exchange, promissory notes, negotiable instruments;
   - the statutory contract under s14 Companies Act 1985;
   - contracts of employment;
   - agency contracts.

10. The Act will have a number of effects.

- Many third parties' rights gained under a contract will be enforceable.
- Many exceptions to the doctrine become unnecessary, e.g. claimants in *Beswick v Beswick, Tweddle v Atkinson, Jackson v Horizon Holidays*, etc. would all have a valid claim under the Act because contracts in each case were creating an express right in their favour.
- Third parties will also find it much easier to rely on the protection of exclusion clauses that include them.
- Not all of the exceptions could fall within the Act, e.g. collateral contracts.
- Parties may simply exclude the Act and so would still be caught by the doctrine.
- The exact scope of s1(1)(b) will only be established in subsequent case law.

CHAPTER 4

THE CONTENTS OF THE CONTRACT

4.1 REPRESENTATIONS

1. Before formation parties identify the basis they wish to contract on.
2. Any statement of fact made at this stage is a 'representation'.
3. A term is a representation either expressly incorporated into the contract or implied by fact or by law.
4. It is therefore distinguished from other representations as it forms part of the contract and can be relied on.
5. Representations are of more or less significance to the parties.
6. The types of representation must be distinguished because the existence and character of liability depends on the type.

Type	If liability is created	Reason
Terms	Create binding obligations so attach liability (and range of remedies if breached).	Actually incorporated into the contract and so are the obligations under it.
Mere representations	Attach no liability in themselves if correctly stated.	Induce a party to enter a contract but do not become part of it – so not binding.
Mis-representations	Can attach liability (and range of remedies depending on how they are made – compare *Derry v Peek* with *Howard Marine & Dredging Co. v Ogden*).	Even though not part of the contract the representation did act to induce the other party to enter the contract and so vitiated their free will.
Mere opinions	Attach no liability in themselves (*Bisset v Wilkinson*).	Opinion is not a matter of fact and is variable.
Expert opinions	Can attach liability (as terms if important enough to be incorporated), or as misrepresentations if falsely stated (*Esso v Marden*).	Because we are entitled to rely, and do rely, on the skill and expertise of experts.
Trade puffs	Attach no liability.	Mere advertising boasts so we are deemed not to take them seriously.
Puffs with an attached promise	May attach liability (*Carlill v Carbolic Smoke Ball Co.*).	Because, although made in connection with a mere puff, the promise is sufficiently specific to be relied upon.

The consequences of different types of representation

Incorporating express terms

A representation is only binding if incorporated as an express term of the contract.

Incorporation is likely where:

- the representation is identified as important to one party (*Birch v Paramount Estates*);
- one party relies on the expertise of the other party (*Dick Bentley v Harold Smith Motors*);
- the statement and the making of the contract are close in time (*Routledge v McKay*);
- the contract is in writing;
- the contract is signed (*L'Estrange v Graucob*).

Implied terms

Terms can be implied by fact, e.g.

- by custom (*Hutton v Warren*);
- by past dealings (*Hillas v Arcos*);
- to make sense of the agreement (*Schawel v Reade*);
- for business efficacy (*The Moorcock*).

This is based on the presumed intention of the parties – measured by the 'officious bystander' test in *Shirlaw v Southern Foundries*.

Terms can also be implied by statute, e.g.

- Sale of Goods Act 1979;
- Equal Pay Act 1970.

TERMS

Construction of terms

- Implied terms are construed according to how they are described.
- With express terms, if the type of term is identified the judges usually give effect to the expressed intent of the parties.
- However, the term must be accurately described (*Schuler v Wickman*).
- If the contract is silent on the type of term then judges try to construe the intent of the parties.

The relative significance of terms

- Terms can be of two types.
  a) Conditions – 'go to the root of the contract', so on breach have remedies available of repudiation and/or sue for damages (*Poussard v Spiers*).
  b) Warranties – generally descriptive terms, so only remedy on breach is to sue for damages (*Bettini v Gye*).
- Now there is also the innominate term – look for seriousness of breach (*Hong Kong Fir Shipping v Kawasaki Kisen Kaisha*).
- Very appropriate in the case of technical breaches (*Reardon Smith Line v Hansen Tangen*).

4.2 TERMS

4.2.1 The nature of terms

1. Terms are the contents or subject matter of the contract.
2. So they are binding obligations which the parties agree to perform in order for the contract to be complete.
3. If either party fails to comply with the obligations they have set themselves there is breach of contract and potential legal action.
4. Terms derive from negotiations preceding formation of the contract, or may be inserted into the contract by other means.
5. In this way terms can be:
   - expressly stated and incorporated into the contract by the parties themselves;
   - implied factually from the circumstances as being the presumed intention of the parties;
   - imputed into the contract by process of law for some other purpose, e.g. for consumer protection.

4.2.2 Incorporating express terms into the contract

1. Not all representations become terms of the contract.
2. If the contract is written it is easier to determine which is a term.
3. The courts have devised tests to determine whether or not the representation is incorporated into the contract as a term.
4. If not it may still be actionable misrepresentation if falsely stated.
5. Many factors can be considered in testing incorporation:
   (a) the importance attached to the representation by one party:
       - the greater the importance attached the more likely it is to be a term (*Birch v Paramount Estates* (1956));

●particularly if the purpose is defeated if the representation cannot be relied upon (*Couchman v Hill* (1947)).

(b) the level of expertise of the representor:

●if one party relies on the other party's skill and judgment then it is likely to be a term (*Dick Bentley Productions Ltd. v Harold Smith (Motors) Ltd.* (1965));

●but a representation made without skill or expertise is less likely to be a term (*Oscar Chess Ltd. v Williams* (1957)).

(c) the time span between the representation and formation of the contract – a longer gap and the representation is unlikely to be seen as a term (*Routledge v McKay*);

(d) whether the representation was in a written agreement;

(e) whether a written agreement was signed – parties are taken to agree to everything they sign even if they do not read it (*L'Estrange v Graucob* (1934));

(f) a representation will not become a term unless the party subject to it was aware of it at the time of contracting (*Olley v Marlborough Court Hotel Ltd.* (1949)). The term must be sufficiently drawn to the notice of the party subject to it for it to be relied on (*O'Brien v MGN Ltd* (2001)).

(g) in oral contract, terms from standard form contracts cannot be binding unless the buyer is made aware of them (*Lidl UK GmbH v Hertford Foods Ltd* (2001)).

4.2.3 The 'parol evidence rule'

1. This rule developed out of the recognition of the difficulties of supplying accurate proof of the terms of simple agreements.
2. Generally oral or other similar evidence that appear to add to, vary, or even contradict the terms of a written agreement would not be recognised as admissible by common law.
3. The reasons for such a rule are relatively obvious and justifiable:

- if the contract was already in writing it was presumed to contain everything that the parties agreed on, and any omissions were not intended to be included;
- adding terms at a later stage only adds to uncertainty.

4. The Law Commission considers the rule unworkable and a number of exceptions to the basic rule have developed:
   (a) custom or trade usage;
   (b) evidence that shows that a contract will not operate until a specified event occurs (*Pym v Campbell* (1856));
   (c) evidence that the agreement is either void or voidable for misrepresentation, mistake, or lack of capacity;
   (d) evidence that the written agreement is in error and that rectification should apply (*Webster v Cecil* (1861));
   (e) evidence that the written agreement was not a full and final reflection of the agreement (*J Evans & Son (Portsmouth) Ltd. v Andrea Merzario Ltd.* (1976)).

4.2.4 The process of implying terms into a contract

1. Contracting parties are deemed to include all the terms they wish to be bound by, but sometimes terms are implied.
2. Terms are implied in one of two situations:
   (i) where, in a dispute, the court is trying to give effect to the presumed though unexpressed intentions of the parties – these are called terms implied by fact;
   (ii) where the law demands that certain provisions are included in a contract irrespective of the wishes of the parties – these are called terms implied by law.

4.2.5 Terms implied by fact

1. Courts imply terms into a contract for various reasons including:
   (a) custom – as 'custom hardens into right' (*Hutton v Warren* (1836));

    (b) trade practice or professional custom, e.g. in contracts of marine insurance it is implied that premiums will be paid to the insurer even if the insured defaults;

    (c) to make sense of the agreement (*Schawel v Reade* (1913));

    (d) to conform with prior conduct (*Hillas v Arcos* (1932));

    (e) to preserve 'business efficacy' (*The Moorcock* (1889)).

2. The test of terms implied by fact is the 'officious bystander test' of MacKinnon LJ in *Shirlaw v Southern Foundries Ltd.* (1939) – 'prima facie that which is left to be implied is something so obvious that it goes without saying; so that, if while the parties were making their bargain, an officious bystander were to suggest some express provision they would testily suppress him with a common "Oh of course!"'

3. There are two situations where the test cannot apply:

- if one party is unaware of the term (*Spring v National Amalgamated Stevedores and Dockers Society* (1956));
- if it is uncertain that both parties would have agreed to the term (*Shell (UK) Ltd. v Lostock Garages Ltd.* (1976)).

4. In *Liverpool City Council v Irwin* (1976), Lord Denning said that the appropriate test was merely what was reasonable as between the parties. Lord Cross said it was what was necessary. The Court of Appeal has recently been prepared to accept the use of the 'Wednesbury reasonableness test' in implying terms (*Paragon Finance Plc v Nash* (2001)). See also the House of Lords' approach in *Equitable Life Assurance Society v Hyman* (2000).

4.2.6 Terms implied by common law

1. Judges on occasions will imply a term to regulate a particular type of agreement irrespective of the wishes of the parties.

2. They will do so because of the absence of statutory control of the area (*Liverpool City Council v Irwin* (1976)).

4.2.7 Terms implied by statute

1. Terms are implied by statute where Government chooses to regulate certain types of agreements to protect weaker parties.
2. Terms are implied to redress inequality of bargaining strength.
3. Such terms are enforceable whatever the wishes of the parties.
4. Examples are employment and consumer contracts.
5. In the Sale of Goods Act 1979 consumers are protected by the insertion of the following implied terms.

   - By s12 the implied condition as to title – that the seller has the right to sell the goods (*Rowland v Divall* (1923)).
   - By s13 the implied condition that the goods correspond to any description given to them (*Beale v Taylor* (1967)).
   - By s14(2) the implied condition that the goods are of satisfactory quality – which means that they should be fit for all their normal purposes, free from blemishes and defects and durable (*Rogers v Parish (Scarborough) Ltd* (1987)).
   - By s14(3) the implied condition that the goods are fit for any purpose stated by the buyer – who is thus relying on the skill and judgment of the seller (*Priest v Last* (1903)).
   - By s15 the implied condition that in goods sold by sample the bulk corresponds with the sample (*Godley v Perry* (1960)).

4.2.8 The relative significance of terms

1. Inevitably certain terms are more significant to the contract than others, some being fundamental to the purpose of the contract while others are merely ancillary to the main purpose.
2. The courts have traditionally distinguished them in two ways:

   - their significance to satisfactory completion of the contract;
   - the available remedy or remedies if the term is breached.

3. On this basis the courts have identified two types of term.

   (a) Conditions – terms that 'go to the root of the contract', and are so fundamental that breach would render the contract meaningless. So remedies are for damages and/or repudiation if appropriate (*Poussard v Spiers and Pond* (1876)).

(b) Warranties – minor or ancillary terms and breach would not destroy the purpose of the contract itself, so the available remedy is an action for damages only (*Bettini v Gye* (1876)).

4. Statutory implied terms are identified as either conditions or warranties in the statute itself, e.g. implied conditions in ss12, 13, 14(2), 14(3), and 15 of the Sale of Goods Act. The position (except s12) is modified by s15A Sale and Supply of Goods Act 1994 where, in a non-consumer contract, a breach which is slight in impact may be treated as breach of warranty.

5. Judges have rejected this strict categorisation in developing the concept of the 'innominate term', which aims for the remedy to be fair to both parties.

   (a) In *Hong Kong Fir Shipping Co. Ltd. v Kawasaki Kisen Kaisha Ltd.* Lord Diplock identified that 'some breaches will, and others will not, give rise to an event which will deprive the party not in default of substantially the benefit he was intended to obtain from his contract' the remedy given would 'depend on the nature of the event to which the breach gives rise'.

   (b) So the court should wait and see what the consequences of the breach are in deciding a remedy (*Cehave N.V. v Bremer Handelsgesellschaft dbH (The Hansa Nord)* (1976)).

   (c) Calling terms innominate is effective if the breach is purely technical (*Reardon Smith Line v Hansen Tangen* (1976)).

6. Courts have, however, been prepared to ignore the process and classify terms as conditions, whatever the consequences of the breach, because the circumstances of the case demands it (*Bunge Corporation v Tradex Export Panama* (1980)).

4.2.9 How judges construe terms

1. If a contract states that a term is a condition or warranty then it is generally as simple as following that classification.

2. If the contract is silent the judges will need to construe which

classification is appropriate, which they do as follows:

(a) in the case of a statutory implied term judges follow the standards set by the law;

(b) in the case of an express term where the parties have already classified the term the judges will generally give effect to the expressed intention of the parties;

(c) in the case of express terms which are silent on their classification judges will try to give effect to what they believe is the intention of the parties.

3. However, express classification may be inaccurate since a party can gain advantage by calling every term a condition. In this case judges will construe the term according to how it really operates (*Schuler v Wickman Machine Tool Sales Ltd.* (1973)).

4. In deciding a classification judges may use the commercial context as a guide (*Meredelanto Compania Naviera SA v Bergbau-Handel GmbH (The Mihalis Angelos)* (1970)).

5. A court will generally try to preserve certainty in commercial agreements whatever the express intention of the parties (*Harlingdon and Leinster Enterprises Ltd. v Christopher Hull Fine Art Ltd.* (1990)).

4.3 JUDICIAL CONTROL OF EXCLUSION CLAUSES

4.3.1 Definition and scope of exclusion clauses

1. An exclusion clause (exemption clause) is a term in a contract aiming to exclude the liability of the party inserting it from liability for his/her contractual breaches, or even for torts.

2. A limitation clause restricts or limits the extent of the liability.

3. Both types of clause are harsh on the other party, particularly where that party is of weaker bargaining strength.

4. There was previously no way of avoiding such clauses because of the maxim *caveat emptor* (let the buyer beware) – the other party had to try to negotiate a contract without the clause in. Even the Sale of Goods Act 1893 allowed for such clauses.

Incorporation of the clause into the contract

- A party is bound by a written agreement (s)he has signed (*L'Estrange v Graucob*).
- A party is only bound by a clause that (s)he knew of when the contract was formed (*Olley v Marlborough Court Hotel*).
- Knowledge can be implied from past dealings (*Spurling v Bradshaw*).
- However, actual knowledge is required when past dealings are inconsistent (*McCutcheon v MacBrayne*).
- The party wanting to rely on the clause must properly draw it to the attention of the other party (*Parker v S. E. Railway Co.*).
- A ticket with the clause on the reverse is insufficient (*Chappleton v Barry UDC*).
- Non-specific references to other documents are also insufficient notice (*Dillon v Baltic Shipping Co. (The Mikhail Lermontov)*).
- And the clause may need to be dramatically brought to the other party's attention (*Thornton v Shoe Lane Parking*).
- The rule may apply to other onerous terms, not just exclusion clauses (*Interfoto Picture Library v Stiletto Visual Programmes Ltd.*).

JUDICIAL CONTROL OF EXCLUSION CLAUSES

Other limitations

- Oral misrepresentations about the clause can invalidate it (*Curtiss v Chemical Cleaning Co.*)
- Oral promises can override written terms (*J Evans & Son (Portsmouth) Ltd. v Andrea Merzano Ltd.*).
- Collateral promises can override exclusion clauses (*Webster v Higgin*).
- Third parties cannot rely on protection of an exclusion clause (*Scruttons v Midland Silicones Ltd.*) – but see *New Zealand Shipping v Satterthwaite (The Eurymedon)*.

Construction of the contract

- Even an incorporated clause can fail on construction of the contract as a whole.
- *Contra preferentum* can apply (*Andrews Bros. v Singer*):
  a) any ambiguity works against the party, including the clause (*Hollier v Rambler Motors*);
  b) can apply also to other types of terms (*Vaswani v Italian Motor Cars Ltd.*).
- Where breach is serious standard form terms can be strictly construed (*Computer & System Engineering v John Lelliott Ltd.*).
- Originally a 'fundamental breach' was treated as if the whole contract was breached and exclusion clauses could not be relied on (*Karsales v Wallis*):
  a) judges disliked the doctrine (*The Suisse Atlantique case*),
  b) and allow exclusions freely negotiated if bargaining strength is equal (*Photo Productions v Securicor Transport*),
  c) providing the clause is clear and unambiguous (*Ailsa Craig Fishing v Malvern Fishing*),
  d) though a clause may be measured against statutory concepts such as reasonableness (*George Mitchell v Finney Lock Seeds*).

5. The late twentieth century saw moves towards consumer protection, with the courts, statute and European law developing methods to restrict the application of such clauses.
6. Three elements to judicial recognition of exclusion clauses:

- the clause must be actually incorporated into the contract to show that it is part of the contract and can be relied upon;
- construction of the contract must show the clause actually protects the party inserting it for the damage in question, and thus no advantage is gained from doubt or ambiguity;
- other tests may be applied if appropriate.

4.3.2 Incorporation of exclusion clauses

1. Rules on incorporation are interchangeable with those for incorporation of terms generally.
2. Parties are generally bound by the terms of any agreement they have signed (*L'Estrange v Graucob* (1934)).
3. Parties are only bound by an exclusion clause of which they had express knowledge at the time the contract was formed (*Olley v Marlborough Court Hotel* (1949)).

- Parties who have previously contracted on the same terms are deemed to have express knowledge of the clause and so are bound by it (*Spurling v Bradshaw* (1956)).
- However, if past dealings were inconsistent only actual knowledge of the clause is sufficient; it cannot be implied from the past dealings (*McCutcheon v MacBrayne* (1964)).

4. The party seeking to rely on the clause must have effectively brought it to the attention of the other party (*Parker v South Eastern Railway Co.* (1877)).

- Handing over a ticket with reference to the clause on the back is insufficient notice (*Chappleton v Barry UDC* (1952)).
- Unspecific references to the document containing a clause may also be insufficient to incorporate the clause (*Dillon v Baltic Shipping Co. Ltd. (The Mikhail Lermontov)* (1991)).

- The duty to give notice can be strictly interpreted, particularly where the party subject to the clause has little opportunity to negotiate (*Thornton v Shoe Lane Parking* (1971)).
- Strict interpretation has also been applied to clauses that are merely onerous rather than excluding liability (*Interfoto Picture Library v Stiletto Visual Programmes Ltd.* (1988)).

4.3.3 Construction of the contract

1. A successfully incorporated clause can still fail on construction of the contract as a whole.
2. The *contra preferentum* rule may apply, i.e. the phrasing of the clause is ambiguous (*Andrews Bros. (Bournemouth) Ltd. v Singer & Co.* (1934)).

   - Ambiguous expression in the clause works against the party including it in the contract (*Hollier v Rambler Motors* (1972)).
   - The rule is not limited only to construction of exclusion clauses (*Vaswani v Italian Motor Cars Ltd.* (1996)).

3. Clauses in standard form contracts may be strictly construed to invalidate them when the breach is serious (*Computer & System Engineering plc v John Lelliott Ltd.* (1991)).
4. Originally, by the doctrine of 'fundamental breach', an exclusion clause might be inoperable because breach of a fundamental term was said to be breach of the whole contract (*Karsales (Harrow) v Wallis* (1956)).

   (a) However, this was destructive to freedom of contract, so it was not always applied (*Suisse Atlantique Societé d'Aramament Maritime SA v NV Rotterdamsche Kolen Centrale (The Suisse Atlantique case)* (1967)).
   (b) Courts accepted that an exclusion clause or a limitation clause could be enforced if it was freely and genuinely agreed when the contract was formed (*Photo Productions Ltd. v Securicor Transport Ltd.* (1980)).
   (c) Now, if bargaining strength is equal, even with a dramatic breach, if the clause is clear and unambiguous then it can

be relied upon (*Ailsa Craig Fishing Co. Ltd. v Malvern Fishing Co. Ltd.* (1983)).

(d) Nevertheless the Court of Appeal has recently identified that, where one clause accepting liability and one limiting or excluding liability for specific types of damage are mutually contradictory, even though one clause appears to cover the type of loss suffered, the clause may fail for ambiguity (*The University of Keele v Price Waterhouse* (2004)).

(e) Since the Unfair Contract Terms Act 1977 courts might apply the test of reasonableness from the Act (*George Mitchell Ltd. v Finney Lock Seeds Ltd.* (1983)).

(f) Courts are in any case reluctant to intervene where a clause in standard forms is challenged but is based on well known, long standing and accepted trade practice (*Overland Shoes Ltd v Schenkers Ltd* (1998)).

4.3.4 Other limitations on the use of exclusion clauses

1. Oral misrepresentations about the scope of an exclusion clause in a written contract may invalidate the clause as it is the misrepresentation that is relied upon (*Curtiss v Chemical Cleaning Co. Ltd.* (1951)).

2. Terms (and exclusion clauses) can be overridden by oral promises made before the contract was formed (*J Evans & Son (Portsmouth) Ltd. v Andrea Merzario Ltd.* (1976)).

3. As can collateral undertakings (*Webster v Higgin* (1948)).

4. Generally, contracts only bind the parties involved so that an exclusion clause will not protect a third party from liability (*Scruttons v Midland Silicones Ltd.* (1962)).

5. However, some inroads into this principle have allowed third parties to contracts to bring themselves within the scope of the exclusion (*New Zealand Shipping Co. Ltd. v Satterthwaite & Co. Ltd. (The Eurymedon)* (1975)).

Clauses void under UCTA

Excluding liability for:

- death/personal injury;
- breaches of implied terms under ss12–15 Sale of Goods Act in consumer contract;
- breaches of implied terms under ss3–5 in Sale & Supply of Goods Act 1982 in consumer contracts;
- any similar provisions in the Consumer Credit Act 1974.

Definition of consumer in UCTA

- One party contracts not in the course of a business, or not holding himself out as carrying out a business.
- The other party contracts in the course of a business.
- The goods are of a kind that are ordinarily supplied for private use or consumption.

STATUTORY CONTROL OF EXCLUSION CLAUSES

Unfair Terms in Consumer Contract Regulations 1999

- Applies to all consumer contracts.
- Applies to any unfair term.
- Provides range of examples of imbalances.
- Aims to remove any unfairness.

Contracts valid if reasonable under UCTA

Excluding liability for:

- loss other than injury caused by negligence;
- a different performance or no performance in consumer or standard form contracts;
- breaches of implied terms under ss13–15 Sale of Goods Act 1979 in business dealings;
- breaches of the implied terms in the Supply of Goods & Services Act 1982 in business dealings;
- misrepresentations.

Test of reasonableness in UCTA

Means reasonable in the light of the knowledge of the parties when they are contracted.

Factors to consider:

- Was there comparable bargaining strength?
- Did the buyer receive any inducement?
- Were the goods manufactured, processed or adapted to meet buyer's own specifications?
- Does trade custom apply?

4.4 STATUTORY CONTROL OF EXCLUSION CLAUSES

4.4.1 The scope of statutory regulation

1. Judge-made rules were traditionally used to control the use of unfair exclusions of liability in contracts.
2. Now the most effective control is found in statutory provisions, which in turn have been recently modified to comply with EU law.
3. The law is found in:

   - The Unfair Contract Terms Act 1977;
   - The Unfair Terms in Consumer Contracts Regulations 1999.

4. UCTA seriously curtails freedom of contract, and also applies to exclusions for torts as well as breaches of contract.
5. The 1999 Regulations replaced the Unfair Terms in Consumer Contracts Regulations 1994 which gave effect to EU Directive 93/13 on unfair terms.

   - The 1999 Regulations are closer to the Directive's wording.
   - The Directive's key objective was producing harmonious rules to replace widely divergent national ones.
   - The Regulations are narrower than UCTA as they only apply to consumers.
   - They are broader than UCTA as they apply to unfair terms generally, not just exclusions, and they impose stricter duties.

4.4.2 The Unfair Contract Terms Act 1977

Introduction

1. This is a most significant area of consumer protection.
2. It does not, however, cover every type of exclusion or unfair term, but can apply sometimes even where there is no contract.
3. It compensates for inequality in bargaining strength by:

   - making certain exclusion clauses automatically void;
   - distinguishing between consumer and inter-business contracts;

- introducing a test of reasonableness to be applied in the case of the latter and in the case of some standard forms.

Exclusions rendered void by the Act

1. Certain types of exclusion clauses are invalid and cannot be relied upon by the person inserting them in the contract.
   - By s2(1) there can be no valid exclusion for death or injury caused by the negligence of the party inserting the clause.
   - By s5(1), in any consumer contract a clause excluding liability by reference to the terms of a guarantee fails in respect of defects caused by negligence in manufacture or distribution.
   - By s6(1) exclusion for breach of s12 Sale of Goods Act 1979 (the implied condition as to title) is invalid.
   - By s6(2), in any consumer contract any exclusion for breach of any of the implied conditions in the Sale of Goods Act s13 (description), s14(2) (satisfactory quality), s14(3) (fitness for the purpose), and s15 (sale by sample) is invalid.
   - Breaches of conditions in Schedule 4 Consumer Credit Act 1974 (similar to those in Sale of Goods Act) are also invalid.
   - By s7(1) the same applies in respect of goods supplied under the Supply of Goods and Services Act 1982.
2. Also under the Consumer Protection Act 1987 there can be no valid exclusion for breaches of the general safety standards.

The distinction between consumer contracts and business contracts

1. The Act operates predominantly for the protection of consumers.
2. Consumer contract is defined in s12(1) as where:
   - one party contracts not in the course of a business, or not holding himself out as carrying out a business;
   - the other party does contract in the course of a business;
   - the goods are of a kind that are ordinarily supplied for private use or consumption.

3. A person claiming to be a business to gain trade discount loses the protection of s12 and cannot claim to be a consumer.
4. By s14 business includes profession, central or local government.
5. By s12(3) it is for the party seeking to rely on the clause to disprove that it is a consumer contract.

Exclusions only valid if reasonable

The Act identifies a number of exclusions that will only be valid if they satisfy a test of reasonableness.

1. By s2(2) there is an exclusion for loss other than death or injury caused by the negligence of the party inserting the clause.
2. By s3, when one party deals as a consumer on the other party's standard forms exclusion for breach, a substantially different performance, or for no performance at all.
3. By s6(3) there are exclusions for breaches of the implied conditions in s13, s14(2), s14(3) and s15 Sale of Goods Act 1979 in inter-business contracts.
4. By s7(3) there are exclusions for breaches of the implied conditions in the Supply of Goods and Services Act in s3, s4, and s5.
5. By s8 there are exclusions for misrepresentations.
6. By s4 there are indemnity clauses – compare (*Thompson v T H Lohan (Plant Hire) Ltd. & J W Hurdiss Ltd.* (1987)) with (*Philips Products Ltd. v Hyland* (1987)).

The test of reasonableness

1. The Act does not define what is reasonable, but guidelines are set out in both s11 and in Schedule 2.
2. By s11(5) the burden of proving that the clause is reasonable is on the party wishing to rely on it (*Warren v Trueprint* (1986)).
3. There are in fact three tests:
   (a) by s11(1) one test is 'was including the clause reasonable in the light of the knowledge of the parties on contracting?';

(b) by s11(2) for exclusions falling under either s6(3) or s7(3) criteria in Schedule 2 should be considered:
- Was there comparable bargaining strength?
- Did the buyer receive any inducement or advantage?
- Were the goods manufactured or processed or adapted to meet the buyer's own specifications?
- Should the buyer have expected an exclusion clause based on trade custom? (*Thompson v T Lohan (Plant Hire) Ltd and J W Hurdiss Ltd* (1987)).

(c) by s11(4), in the case of limitation clauses the ability of the party relying on the clause to meet liability if necessary or to insure against it should also be considered.

4. Judges are willing to apply the criteria in Schedule 2 to exclusions and limitations generally (*George Mitchell v Finney Lock Seeds* (1983)) and (*Smith v Eric S Bush* (1990)).

Contracts falling outside the scope of the Act

Certain contracts are not covered by the provisions of the Act:
- contracts of insurance (which in any case are based on risk);
- contracts to create, transfer or terminate interests in land;
- contracts for patents, copyrights, or other intellectual property;
- contracts for the creation or dissolution of companies;
- contracts of marine salvage, charter-parties, and carriage of goods.

4.4.3 The Unfair Terms in Consumer Contracts Regulations 1999

The scope and purpose of the regulations

1. Article 7(1) of Directive 93/13 requires that 'adequate and effective means exist to prevent the continued use of unfair terms in contracts concluded with consumers'.
2. The Regulations seek to achieve this by:
   - applying to unfair terms generally, not just exclusion clauses;
   - declaring invalid and non-binding any term found to be

'unfair' – although the rest of the contract can bind if it can continue without that term (Regulation 8);

- providing a non-exhaustive list of examples of unfair terms in Schedule 2;
- providing the means for the Director General of Fair Trading to consider complaints (Regulation 10) – powers also exist for the 'qualifying bodies' to take action, e.g. the directors general of electricity, gas and water, rail regulator, weights and measures authorities, and Consumer's Association.

3. The Regulations apply only to consumer contracts.

- A consumer contract is defined in Regulation 4 as one made between a seller/supplier and a consumer.
- Seller/supplier is defined as 'any person who sells or supplies goods or services and who, in making a contract, is acting for purposes related to his business'.
- Consumer is defined as 'any natural person ... acting for purposes ... outside his trade, business or profession'.

4. By Regulation 5 a term is unfair that is not individually negotiated and is contrary to good faith (i.e. in standard forms). The House of Lords in *Director General of Fair Trading v First National Bank plc* (2002) has held that 'good faith' covers only procedural unfairness, though Lord Steyn, dissenting, thought it should refer to any 'significant imbalance' in substance also.

5. Regulation 6 identifies that the legislature is not concerned with the fairness of core terms such as price.

6. Regulation 7 is the *contra preferentum* rule in statutory form – the words of a term must be in 'plain intelligible language' and any ambiguity is construed in favour of the consumer.

Terms regarded as unfair under Schedule 2

The list is generally non-exhaustive, but includes those which:

- exclude liability for death or personal injury;
- inappropriately limit liability for inadequate performance or non-performance, or which exclude a right of set off;

- are binding on the consumer but optional to the seller;
- allow the seller to keep a deposit in the event of the consumer's cancellation, but not the other way round;
- make a consumer in breach pay excessive compensation;
- allow the seller to terminate the contract, but not the buyer;
- allow the seller to end the contract without reasonable notice – except where there are serious grounds for doing so;
- automatically extend a fixed-term contract when the deadline for the consumer to object is unreasonably early;
- irrevocably bind the consumer to terms he had no means to discover before the contract was made;
- allow the seller to unilaterally vary terms without a valid reason specified in the contract;
- allow the seller to unilaterally vary the character of the product or service supplied without a valid reason;
- allow for price to be determined on delivery or for the seller to alter the price without letting the consumer cancel;
- give the seller the sole right to interpret the contract or to determine whether goods conform to the contract;
- limit the sellers obligations for his agents' promises;
- oblige the consumer to fulfil all obligations, but not the seller;
- give sellers the right, without agreement of the consumer, to transfer obligations which might then reduce the rights of the consumer under guarantees;
- exclude consumers' rights to take legal action, or restrict evidence available to consumers, or alter the burden of proof.

CHAPTER 5
VITIATING FACTORS

5.1 VOID AND VOIDABLE CONTRACTS

5.1.1 The nature of vitiating factors

1. The fact that a contract has all the necessary requirements of valid formation does not mean that the contract is perfect.
2. The requirements of formation – offer, acceptance, consideration, and intention are technical requirements and a contract may still be unenforceable because of other defects, hidden at formation which, if known to both parties at the time, may have resulted in no contract being formed.
3. These defects are called vitiating factors, and a contract affected by them is sometimes called an imperfect contract.
4. A vitiating factor, once discovered, may invalidate an otherwise validly formed contract because the agreement lacks the necessary voluntariness on both sides.
5. The different vitiating factors operate in one of two ways:
   - the contract is void, i.e. never valid from the start;
   - the contract is voidable, i.e. may be avoided by one party.

5.1.2 Void contracts

1. A void contract is as if the contract had not been formed.
2. This is because the nature of the vitiation means that a valid contract could never have been formed.
3. The effect is to taint and perhaps invalidate related transactions.

5.1.3 Voidable contracts

1. The contract is not automatically terminated, as a void contract is.
2. A party affected by the vitiating factor can end the contract or continue with it if it would be to his/her benefit to do so.
3. Alternatively they can replace the terms with more preferable ones.

5.2 MISREPRESENTATION

5.2.1 Introduction

Misrepresentation defined
Misrepresentation is:
- a falsely made statement of material fact, not opinion (*Bisset v Wilkinson*), nor future intention (*Edgington v Fitzmaurice*), nor trade puffs (*Carlill v Carbolic Smoke Ball Co.*);
- made by one party to the other party, not by a third party (*Peyman v Lanjani*);
- before formation, not after (*Roscoria v Thomas*);
- intended to induce the other party to enter the contract; but not to form part of it.

Classes of misrepresentation and remedies
Fraudulent misrepresentation:
- brought under the tort of deceit;
- must be made deliberately or knowingly, without belief in truth, or carelessly (*Derry v Peek*);
- so, defence merely = honest belief.
Remedies:
- sue for damages under tort measure, including all consequential loss (*Smith New Court Securities v Scrimgeour*);
- affirm contract, or disaffirm and use as defence to claim of breach, or seek rescission in equity.
Negligent misrepresentation:
- sue in tort under *Hedley Byrne* where there is a 'special relationship';
- sue under s2(1) Misrepresentation Act (*Howard Marine Dredging v Ogden*);
- Remedy = damages (tort measure).
Innocent misrepresentation:
- sue under s2(2) for damages or seek rescission.

MISREPRESENTATION

Non-disclosure
No basic common law duty to disclose information not requested (*Fletcher v Krell*).
But exceptions are:
- *uberimmae fides* (utmost good faith), *Locker & Woolf v Western Australian Insurance Co.*;
- part truth (*Dimmock v Hallett*);
- true statement becomes false (*With v O'Flannagan*)

Equity and misrepresentation
Contract voidable yet not void, so rescission possible if:
- *restitutio in integrum* possible (*Lagunas Nitrate v Lagunas Syndicate*);
- contract affirmed (*Long v Lloyd*);
- no excessive delay (*Leaf v International Galleries*);
- third party rights gained (*Car & Universal Finance v Caldwell*).
Indemnity is also possible (*Whittington v Seale-Hayne*).

1. The 'representations' made prior to formation can become terms if incorporated, or will remain outside of the contract.
2. 'Mere representations' on their own have no contractual significance. They are used to induce the other party to enter the contract, but if accurately stated create no liability.
3. Only a falsely stated or inaccurate representation is actionable.
4. The motive behind the falsehood is not vital to establishing that a misrepresentation exists, though it can be critical to determine the class of misrepresentation, and thus the remedies available.
5. If misrepresentation is established the contract is voidable, and the victim of the misrepresentation may avoid his/her obligations under the contract or have the contract set aside.
6. There are many practical considerations to remember.

   ● Traditionally there were virtually no remedies available, so it was vital to prove that the false representation was incorporated as a term.
   ● Misrepresentation is a fairly new class of action created in statute, although there are some limited common law possibilities either through tort or in equity.
   ● Misrepresentation is close in character to common mistake. The latter is sometimes preferred because a successful claim makes the contract void rather than voidable.

5.2.2 Misrepresentation defined

1. A misrepresentation is:
   (a) a statement of material fact;
   (b) made by one party to a contract to the other party;
   (c) before or at the time of formation of the contract;
   (d) was intended to act as an inducement to the other party to enter the contract, and was such an inducement;
   (e) but not intended as a binding obligation of the contract;
   (f) and was falsely or incorrectly stated.

2. If any of these requirements is not present then the representation complained of is not a misrepresentation.

3. A statement of material fact must not be:

   (a) a mere opinion (*Bisset v Wilkinson* (1927));

   (b) an expression of future intent (unless it falsely represents a current state of mind) (*Edgington v Fitzmaurice* (1885));

   (c) a mere trade puff (on the maxim *simplex commendatio non obligat*) (*Carlill v Carbolic Smoke Ball Co.* (1893)).

4. But the misrepresentation can result from conduct rather than being oral or in writing (*Spice Girls Ltd v Aprilia World Service BV* (2000)).

5. Anything said by a third party (except an agent of a party) cannot be a misrepresentation (*Peyman v Lanjani* (1985)).

6. A statement made after formation is not actionable (*Roscorla v Thomas* (1842)).

7. To be an inducement to the other party the representation must:

   ● be materially important to the making of the contract (*JEB Fasteners Ltd. v Mark Bloom & Co.* (1983));

   ● and the party must actually be induced (*Museprime Properties Ltd. v Adhill Properties Ltd.* (1990)).

8. To be an inducement the representation must not:

   (a) remain unknown to the other party;

   (b) already be known as false by the other party;

   (c) neither be believed nor relied upon (*Attwood v Small* (1838)).

9. If intended to be binding it is likely to be a breach of warranty rather than a misrepresentation (*Couchman v Hill* (1947)).

10. If the representation is accurate then the contract is complete.

5.2.3 Classes of misrepresentation and their remedies

Introduction

1. Misrepresentations vary from telling deliberate lies to innocently repeating inaccurate information.

2. Originally, with no remedy available for misrepresentation, it was vital to prove incorporation and thus breach of a term.
3. Prior to the 1967 Act there was some development in tort and in equity, but not contract law itself.
4. So the significance of the class of misrepresentation was in how it could be proved and what remedy was available.
5. The significance lessened after the Misrepresentation Act 1967.

Fraudulent misrepresentation

1. This was originally the only available common law action.
2. It was brought in the tort of deceit and was only available if fraud could be proved.
3. Fraud was defined in *Derry v Peek* (1889) by Lord Herschell as where the false representation was made either:

  - knowingly or deliberately; or
  - without belief in its truth; or
  - recklessly, without caring whether it was true or not.

4. So the best defence is to show an honest belief, which need not be reasonable, merely honestly held, so fraud is very hard to prove.
5. The motive for fraud is irrelevant (*Akerhielm v De Mare* (1959)).
6. Recklessness is only evidence of fraud, not proof, unless it amounts to blatant disregard for the truth and so is also dishonest (*Thomas Witter Ltd. v TBP Industries Ltd.* (1996)).

The remedies for fraudulent misrepresentation

1. By suing in the tort of deceit the measure of damages is in tort.
2. According to Lord Denning, remoteness does not apply as 'the defendant is bound to make reparation for all the damage flowing from the fraudulent inducement' *(Doyle v Olby (Ironmongers) Ltd.* (1969)).

3. The test of damages is now in *Smith New Court Securities Ltd. v Scrimgeour Vickers (Asset Management) Ltd.* (1996).

- The defendant is responsible for all damages, including any consequential loss, provided that there is a causal link between the misrepresentation and damage.
- This results in heavier claims so encourages fraud actions.

4. Where suing for damages the claimant can also:

- affirm the contract and continue with it; or
- disaffirm the contract and refuse any further performance.

5. There are two other possibilities if the claimant refuses further performance:

- take no action if no advantage is to be gained, but use the fraud as a defence to the other party's counterclaim (and the claimant may refuse to return, e.g. insurance premiums paid);
- seek rescission of the contract in equity.

Negligent misrepresentation

1. Traditionally all non-fraudulent misrepresentations were classed as innocent, with no common law action or remedy.

2. Now actions are available both at common law and by statute.

3. At common law.

(a) An action for negligent misstatement causing a pecuniary (financial) loss was established in *Hedley Byrne v Heller & Partners* (1964). (Approved Lord Denning's dissenting judgment in *Candler v Crane Christmas & Co.* (1951)).

(b) Liability only arises if the representor owes a duty of care to the representee, so a 'special relationship' must exist.

(c) The appropriate test for liability requires:

(i) possession of a particular type of knowledge by the defendant (*Harris v Wyre Forest DC* (1988));

(ii) proximity between the parties (not necessarily contractual) (*Caparo Industries v Dickman* (1990));

(iii) the defendant is aware that the claimant is relying on the advice given (*Chaudhry v Prabhakar* (1988)).

(d) The principle may also cover representations as to a future state of affairs (*Esso Petroleum Co. Ltd. v Marden* (1976)).

4. By statute.

(a) Statutory liability is in the Misrepresentation Act 1967 s2(1) – if, as a result of a misrepresentation, a person has suffered loss then the person making it is liable for damages even though it was not made fraudulently, unless (s)he can show (s)he had reasonable grounds to believe in the statement.

(b) There are a number of consequences to the Act:

- the burden of proof is reversed;
- the claimant can choose the Act or common law;
- there is no need to show a special relationship under the Act (*Howard Marine Dredging Co. Ltd. v A Ogden & Sons (Excavating) Ltd.* (1978)).

Remedies for negligent misrepresentation

1. Damages are available under both the Act and common law.

2. At common law it is the tort measure, based on foreseeable loss.

3. The Act uses a tort measure, but it is uncertain whether it is that in the tort of deceit (*Royscott Trust Ltd. v Rogerson* (1991)).

4. Damages can be reduced for contributory negligence.

5. Traditionally all non-fraudulent misrepresentation was classed as innocent and the only remedy would be rescission in equity.

Innocent misrepresentation

1. Innocent misrepresentation after the Act probably only refers to repeating inaccurate information honestly believing it to be true.

2. No common law action, but rescission always possible in equity.

3. Now, if s2(1) is not available, there is the possibility of damages under s2(2) as an alternative to rescission.

Remedies for innocent misrepresentation

1. Since damages would not be available at common law they are not available under s2(1) either.
2. But damages are available under s2(2) if rescission is possible.
3. So four points can be made:
   - there is no absolute, only a discretionary, right to damages;
   - damages is instead of, not as well as rescission, so if right to rescission is lost there is no right to damages either (*Zanzibar v British Aerospace (Lancaster House) Ltd* (2000));
   - the measure of damages is uncertain;
   - an innocent misrepresentation may be incorporated which may give claimant rights as terms (*Watts v Spence* (1975)).
4. Rescission, the only former remedy, was granted because 'no man ought to be able to take advantage of his own false statements' – Sir George Jessel in *Redgrave v Hurd* (1881).

5.2.4 Equity and misrepresentation

1. An actionable misrepresentation makes the contract voidable not void, so the contract is valid until set aside by one party.
2. Rescission is available whatever class of misrepresentation, but:
   - it is a discretionary remedy;
   - the court must consider the degree of seriousness of the breach and the likely consequences of rescission.
3. The right to rescind may be lost in certain circumstances:
   - if *restitutio in integrum* is impossible (if the parties cannot be restored to their pre-contractual position) (*Lagunas Nitrate Co. v Lagunas Syndicate* (1899));
   - if the contract is affirmed (*Long v Lloyd* (1958));
   - if there is excessive delay (*Leaf v International Galleries* (1950));
   - if a third party has gained rights in the property (*Car and Universal Finance Co. Ltd. v Caldwell* (1964));
   - if, under s2(2) the court feels that damages is the more appropriate remedy.

4. It is possible to recover an indemnity at the same time as rescission (*Whittington v Seale-Hayne* (1900)).

5.2.5 Non-disclosure as misrepresentation

1. No basic common law obligation to disclose information not requested by the other party (*Fletcher v Krell* (1873)).
2. Silence on its own need not, therefore, be misrepresentation (*Hands v Simpson, Fawcett & Co.* (1928)).
3. Sometimes withholding of information is actionable:

- contracts *uberimmae fides* (those where the utmost good faith is required) (*Locker and Wool v Western Australian Insurance Co.* (1936));
- contracts involving fiduciary relationships (*Tate v Williamson* (1866));
- where part truth is falsehood (*Dimmock v Hallett* (1866));
- where a true statement becomes false during the negotiations and the other side is not informed (*With v O'Flannagan* (1936)).

5.3 MISTAKE

Common mistake
Same mistake made by both parties.
If operative then contract void.
Can be:
- mistake as to existence of subject matter (*Couturier v Hastle*);
- mistake as to ownership of subject matter (*Cooper v Phibbs*).

A mistake as to the quality of the contract has no effect – contract continues (*Bell v Lever Bros.*).

Mutual mistake
The parties are at cross-purposes.
- Court will try and find a common intention.
- If promises are entirely contradictory then mistake is operative and contract void (*Raffles v Wichelhaus*).
- Ambiguity may make the contract void (*Scriven v Hindley*).
- But the mistake is not operative if only one party mistaken and performance is possible (*Smith v Hughes*).

Non est factum
Where one party signs a document by mistake.
To avoid it:
- document must be different to what it was represented as;
- no negligence in signing (*Saunders v Anglia Building Society*).

MISTAKE

Unilateral mistake
Only one party is mistaken and the other party is taking advantage of it.
Mistake over terms – contract operative and void if:
- party genuinely mistaken on a material detail and would not have contracted;
- other party should have known;
- mistaken party not at fault (*Sybron Corporation v Rochem*).

Mistaken identity – contract operative and void if:
- mistaken party intended to contract with someone different (*Kings Norton Metal case*);
- mistake was material to formation of contract (*Cundy v Lindsay*);
- mistake was known to other party (*Boulton v Jones*).

Mistaken identity face-to-face:
- party deemed to intend to contract with person present – mistake is only to creditworthiness (*Lewis v Avery*).

Mistake and equity
Possible only if mistake not operable – can:
- rescind (*Solle v Butcher*);
- refuse specific performance (*Webster v Cecil*);
- rectify a document (*Craddock v Hunt*).

5.3.1 Introduction

1. There are three classes of mistake.

- Common mistake – both parties make the same mistake.
- Mutual mistake – the parties are at cross purposes.
- Unilateral mistake – only one party is mistaken and the other party knows of the mistake and takes advantage of it.

2. Common mistake may make performance impossible; mutual mistake and unilateral mistake may have no *consensus ad idem*.

3. The main question is the effect on the contract, and whether common law or equity applies.

- If the mistake is 'operative' (i.e. it is why the contract was made or is fundamental to the contract) then the common law applies and the contract is void *ab initio*.
- Only if the mistake is not operative may equity provide a remedy for the victim, and that party can avoid the contract.

5.3.2 The classes of mistake

Common mistake

1. There are three types with differing consequences.

2. *Res extincta.*

(a) If, at the time of the contract, unknown to both parties, the subject matter of the contract had been destroyed then the contract is void (*Couturier v Hastie* (1852)).

(b) If there is no guarantee that the subject matter exists the mistake does not effect the contract (*McRae v Commonwealth Disposals* (1950)).

(c) If the goods commercially perished rather than ceased to exist the mistake is operative and the contract void (*Barrow Lane and Ballard Ltd. v Phillip Phillips & Co. Ltd.* (1929)).

3. *Res sua.*

(a) The mistake is over who actually owns the contract property.

(b) A contract is void if a party contracts for something neither party realises he already owns (*Cooper v Phibbs* (1867)).

4. Mistake as to the quality of the contract made.

(a) If the common mistake concerns the anticipated quality then the mistake:
   (i)   is not operative;
   (ii) has no effect on the contract;
   (iii) and the parties are bound by their original obligations.

(b) If the mistake is not 'of such a fundamental character as to constitute an underlying assumption without which the parties would not have made the contract they in fact made ...' (Lord Warrington). (*Bell v Lever Brothers* (1932)).

(c) The rule can cause problems where mistake as to quality is common: compare *Leaf v International Galleries* (1950) and *Peco Arts Inc. v Hazlitt Gallery Ltd* (1983). In both cases the mistake was about the authenticity of paintings. The two conflict over whether or not this is an operative mistake.

Mutual mistake

1. The parties are at cross purposes over the meaning of the contract, so doubtful if a meaningful agreement was reached.

2. The court tries to 'make sense' of the agreement and to maintain it if they can objectively find a common intent.

3. But where promises are so contradictory as to make performance impossible, then the mistake is operative and the contract is void (*Raffles v Wichelhaus* (1864)).

4. Ambiguity surrounding the subject matter may make the contract void (*Scriven Bros. & Co. v Hindley & Co.* (1913)).

5. The contract is not voided if one party only mistakes the contract quality and performance is possible (*Smith v Hughes* (1871)).

Unilateral mistake

1. Mistake as to the terms of the contract.

(a) If a party makes a material mistake expressing his/her intent and the other party knows, or is deemed to know, of it the mistake is operative and the contract void (*Hartog v Colin & Shields* (1939)).

(b) The mistake is operative if:

(i) one party is genuinely mistaken on a material detail, and knowing the truth would not have contracted;

(ii) the other party ought reasonably to have known of the mistake;

(iii) the mistaken party was not at fault (*Sybron Corporation v Rochem Ltd.* (1983)).

(c) So the mistake is not operative if the other party does not know of it (*Wood v Scarth* (1858)).

2. Mistaken identity.

(a) Claimant must prove an intention to contract with a different person, so must prove other person exists (*Kings Norton Metal Co. Ltd. v Edridge, Merrett & Co. Ltd.* (1897)).

(b) The mistake must have been material to the formation of the contract to be operative (*Cundy v Lindsay* (1878)).

(c) For mistake to be material it must be known to the other party (*Boulton v Jones* (1857)).

3. Face-to-face contracting.

(a) A party negotiating a contract in person is deemed to be contracting with the actual person in front of him/her, whatever the identity assumed by the other party (so that person's creditworthiness is not material and cannot be the basis of an operative mistake) – *Phillips v Brooks Ltd.* (1919) and *Lewis v Avery* (1972). But see also Lord Denning in *Ingram v Little* (1960).

(b) To claim that the other party's identity was material requires taking steps to establish their true identity – *Citibank NA*, and *Midland Bank v Brown Shipley & Co. Ltd.* (1991).

(c) Even if the contract is only made through an intermediary without the authority of an agent to bind the party, the rules on face-to-face dealing can still apply (*Shogun Finance Ltd v Hudson* (2003)).

5.3.3 Mistake and equity

1. If a mistake is operative then common law not equity applies.
2. If the mistake is not operative, equity may be used in three ways.

(a) Rescission:
   - available if it would be unconscionable to allow one party to take advantage of the mistake (*Solle v Butcher* (1950));
   - often appropriate in contracts made as the result of an innocent misrepresentation (*Magee v Pennine Insurance Co. Ltd.* (1969));
   - but the Court of Appeal has now suggested that if a common mistake is not operative in common law then neither can the contract be set aside by rescission in equity, in other words that equity has no relevance to common mistake (*Great Peace Shipping Ltd v Tsavliris Salvage (International) Ltd* (2002)).

(b) Refusal of Specific Performance:
   - because an equitable remedy is discretionary;
   - so can be refused where one party entered contract by mistake and:
     (i) it would be unfair to expect him/her to perform; or
     (ii) the mistake was actually caused by the other's misrepresentation; or
     (iii) the other party knew of the mistake and took advantage of it (*Webster v Cecil* (1861));
   - but the order is not refused merely because the mistaken party made a worse bargain (*Tamplin v James* (1880)).

(c) Rectification of a document:
   - court can rewrite document to conform to real agreement;
   - party seeking rectification must prove that:

(i) a complete and certain agreement was reached;

(ii) which remained unchanged to the time of writing (*Craddock v Hunt* (1923)).

5.3.4 Non est Factum

1. Operates only in written agreements – means 'this is not my deed'.

The class of mistake	The character of the mistake	Consequences of the mistake
Common mistake: * *res extincta*	Same mistake made by both parties: * mistake concerns existence of subject matter at time contract made	* Mistake is 'operative' and contract is void
* *res sua*	* mistake is about who owns subject matter at time of contracting	* Mistake is 'operative' and contract is void
* mistake as to quality	* mistake is merely as to quality of bargain made	* Mistake is not 'operative' – contract continues but may be set aside in equity
Mutual mistake	Both parties make a mistake but not the same one – they are at cross purposes	* If performance impossible then contract is void * If court can find common intent then contract may continue
Unilateral mistake: * mistake as to terms	Only one party is mistaken – the other party knows and takes advantage of first party's mistake. * (i) One party mistaken over a material detail; (ii) other party knew of mistake; (iii) mistaken party not at fault.	* If all three, mistake is 'operative' and contract void – if not then may be voidable in equity.
* mistaken identity not face-to-face	* (i) Mistaken party intended to contract with someone else; (ii) mistake material to contract; (iii) mistake known to other party.	* If all three, mistake is 'operative' and contract void – if not then may be voidable in equity.
* mistaken identity face-to-face	* Party contracts in person with someone who claims to be someone else.	* Not an 'operative' mistake – mistaken party deemed to be contracting with person in front of him.
Non est factum	* Mistake concerns nature of document being signed * the document is (i) materially different to what it was represented to be; (ii) there is no negligence by the person signing it.	If both present then there is 'operative' mistake' so contract is void – if not then no effect on contract.

Diagram illustrating the types of mistake and their consequences

Duress

- Must involve a real threat of intimidation, enough to vitiate consent (*Cumming v Ince*).
- So traditionally involves threats of actual violence (*Barton v Armstrong*).

Economic duress

- Such a degree of coercion that the other person is deprived of his/her free consent and agreement (*The Siboen & the Sibotre*).
- Well established in cases of unfair commercial pressure (*Atlas Express v Kafco*).
- Also where external pressure is exerted on businesses, e.g. by trade unions (*The Universal Sentinel*).
- But proving the coercion does not guarantee a remedy (*The Atlantic Baron*).

DURESS AND UNDUE INFLUENCE

Undue influence

- An equitable area involving unfair pressure, coercion vitiating free will.
- Traditional distinction was between:
  - a) actual (where proof of the unfair pressure was required) and
  - b) presumed (where the nature of the relationship meant the party accused of unfair pressure had to disprove it).
- Now, following *Aboody*, the distinction is between:
  - a) Class 1 (actual), where the person alleging the undue influence must also suffer a manifest disadvantage (*Barclays Bank v Coleman*) and
  - b) Class 2A (the old presumed), where the nature of the relationship means undue influence is automatically presumed unless it can be shown that the person alleging it had independent legal advice (*Allcard v Skinner*) and now also
  - c) Class 2B (wives – were formerly excluded from presumed by *National Westminster Bank v Morgan*), where, following *Barclays Bank v O'Brien*, if the claimant can show the relationship was one of trust and confidence then it is for the other party to disprove the undue influence.
- Lending institutes have to be aware of this last class and ensure that they are not caught by a husband's undue influence, so need to ensure that the wife agreeing to stand surety for a loan receives independent legal advice – the rules are now in *Royal Bank of Scotland v Etridge*.

2. Applies to signed contracts (*L'Estrange v Graucob* (1934)), when:
   (a) party signing is subject to a weakness exploited by other party;
   (b) the other party represented the document as something different.

4. For the contract to be void the party signing must take appropriate precautions to establish authenticity of document (*Saunders v Anglian Building Society* (1971)):
   (i) the document is of a kind materially different to what it was represented as being;
   (ii) there is no negligence in signing.

5.4 DURESS, ECONOMIC DURESS AND UNDUE INFLUENCE

5.4.1 Introduction

1. Concerns contracts formed after coercion or unfair pressure.
2. The courts are keen to challenge any type of unfair pressure because to allow contracts made because of pressure to stand would be inconsistent with the principle of freedom of contract.
3. Originally common law recognised a narrow principle of duress.
4. To allow more flexibility equity developed undue influence.
5. In either case a successful plea means the contract is voidable rather than void, and so can be set aside by one party.

5.4.2 Duress

1. An action to avoid a contract was possible originally, if there was intimidation which was sufficiently real and threatening to vitiate consent (*Cumming v Ince* (1847)).
2. So the plea was traditionally associated with threats of violence (*Barton v Armstrong* (1975)).
3. Threats to carry out lawful acts are not duress (*Williams v Bayley* (1886)).
4. So there must be both an unlawful act and one amounting to compulsion vitiating free will (*R v Attorney General of England and Wales* (2003)).

5. The threat must be against the person, not the goods (*Skeate v Beale* (1840)).

6. Although restitution might still be available in the case of the latter (*Maskell v Horner* (1915)).

7. So duress is rare in modern times.

5.4.3 Economic duress

1. More recently courts have developed economic duress to cover situations when commercial viability of a contract is attacked.

2. In *Occidental World-wide Investment Corporation v Skibs A/S Avanti* (1976) *(The Siboen and The Sibotre)*, Lord Kerr identified it as 'such a degree of coercion that the other party was deprived of his free consent and agreement'.

3. In *Pao On v Lau Yiu Long* (1980), Lord Scarman stated that claims depend on 'whether the person alleged to have been coerced did or did not protest ... did or did not have an alternative course open to him ... was independently advised ... took steps to avoid it'.

4. The doctrine has since been successfully applied in *Atlas Express Ltd. v Kafco (Importers and Distributors) Ltd.* (1989).

5. The doctrine has been extended to cover submission to improper pressure by trade unions or federations (*Universe Tankships Inc. of Monrovia v International Transport Workers' Federation (The Universal Sentinel)* (1983)).

   ● However, the difference between unfair pressure and legitimate pressure is unclear (*Dimskal Sipping Co. SA v ITWF (The Evia Luck)* (1991).

   ● It seems a claim is possible even if the threat is one of lawful action (*Alec Lobb (Garages) Ltd. v Total Oil G B Ltd.* (1983)).

6. The doctrine is subject to uncertainty, e.g. it is possible to prove economic duress but be denied a remedy (*North Ocean Co. Ltd. v Hyundai Construction Co. Ltd. (The Atlantic Baron)* (1978)).

5.4.4 Undue influence

Introduction

1. Undue influence is available if there is unfair pressure not covered by the doctrine of duress, so prevents one party taking advantage of the other to gain an unfair advantage.
2. It is governed by equity so any remedy is discretionary.
3. It is a question of degree what influence is appropriate, and for this reason courts have been reluctant to define it.
4. In *Bank of Credit and Commerce International SA v Aboody* (1990) the court distinguished between two classes:

   - Class 1: actual undue influence – the traditional class where parties have no special relationship and the party claiming undue influence must prove it;
   - Class 2: presumed undue influence – the traditional class where a special relationship exists. Some relationships automatically give rise to the presumption, while in others the claimant can show specific facts indicating dominance – the party against whom it is alleged must disprove it.

5. These classifications were accepted in *Barclays Bank plc v O'Brien* (1993) but the House of Lords now doubts whether the classifications are necessary (*Royal Bank of Scotland plc v Etridge (No. 2)* (2001)).

Actual undue influence: Class 1

1. Applies where no special relationship exists, so that it is impossible to argue that an abuse of confidence exists.
2. Claimant must show dominance prevented exercising free will and independently forming contract (*Williams v Bayley* (1866)).
3. First defined as 'some unfair and improper conduct, some coercion from outside, some overreaching, some form of cheating…' (*Allcard v Skinner* (1887)).
4. Extended by Lord Denning to apply in any inequality of bargaining strength (*Lloyds Bank Ltd v Bundy* (1975)). Expressly rejected by HL in *National Westminster Bank plc v*

Morgan (1985): 'an unequal bargain will be a relevant feature in some cases of undue influence. But it can never become an appropriate basis of principle ...' Lord Scarman.

5. *Aboody* required a claimant to show (s)he had suffered a manifest disadvantage – rejected by Lord Browne-Wilkinson in *CIBC Mortgages Ltd. v Pitt* (1993), but apparently resurrected by the CA in *Barclays Bank v Coleman* (2000).

6. Originally included banker and client, and husband and wife (*Midland Bank v Shepherd* (1988)).

7. Now more rare because claimant might show that relationship falls within Class 2B, which then shifts burden of proof.

Presumed undue influence: Class 2

1. Class 2 applies when the claimant can show a relationship of confidence and trust with the party against whom the undue influence is alleged.

2. The claimant only has to prove the relationship – then undue influence is presumed and it is for the defendant to disprove it.

3. To disprove undue influence defendant must show:

   (a) the claimant entered the contract with full knowledge of its nature and effect;

   (b) that the claimant had independent, impartial advice before entering the contract.

4. Traditionally presumed undue influence applied to a number of 'special relationships', which included:

   - all fiduciaries;
   - parents and children (*Lancashire Loans Co. v Black* [1933]);
   - doctors and patients;
   - trustees and beneficiaries (*Benningfield v Baxter* (1886));
   - spiritual leaders and followers (*Allcard v Skinner* (1887)).

5. In *Aboody* CA established that relationships of trust and confidence could arise in one of two ways:

   (a) as above, where the nature of the relationship means undue influence is automatically presumed, e.g. spiritual leaders and followers (*Allcard v Skinner* (1887)) – now regarded as Class 2A);

(b) where no established special relationship exists but the claimant can show the relationship was one of trust and confidence – if this is accepted the presumption of undue influence applies and the defendant must disprove it (now regarded as Class 2B).

6. The most common relationship to fall within Class 2B is husband and wife (*BCCI v Aboody* (1990)), which had been expressly excluded from the special relationships in Class 2A in *Midland Bank v Shepherd* (1988):

* in rare circumstances it can include banker and client (*Lloyds Bank Ltd v Bundy* (1975)) – expressly excluded from Class 2A by *National Westminster Bank plc v Morgan* (1985);
* and might apply wherever the claimant can show a wrongful transaction representing a manifest disadvantage to him/her.

7. The doctrine may apply where the claimant cannot use *non est factum* (*Avon Finance v Bridges* (1985)).

8. If undue influence cannot be shown, misrepresentation or negligence is still possible (*Cornish v Midland Bank plc* (1985)).

The effect of undue influence on third parties

1. Traditionally undue influence involved a person trying to avoid a contract that (s)he was coerced into entering.

2. Modern cases involve the party exercising undue influence so the victim enters a contract with a third party, e.g. husband persuading wife to stand a surety with the bank over his loan.

3. The problem here is lack of privity of contract, meaning that the actions of the wrongdoer will have no effect on the contract.

4. To avoid unfairness, attempts have been made to prevent the enforcement of contracts secured in such ways by adopting one of three arguments:

(a) that the wrongdoer is the agent of the creditor;
(b) a special equity exists to protect the party influenced;
(c) the creditor is bound by the doctrine of notice.

5. Agency and undue influence.

    (a) One argument is that if entry to the contract is secured by the undue influence of the agent, then the principal is also caught by the doctrine and is unable to enforce the contract of surety against the victim (*Kingsnorth Trust Ltd v Bell* (1986)).

    (b) However, this was rejected in *Barclays Bank plc v O'Brien* (1993).

6. Special equitable protection of wives.

    (a) In CA in *O'Brien*, Scott LJ rejected the agency argument and preferred a special equitable protection of wives who give surety for their husband's debts.

    (b) CA held that such a surety would be unenforceable when:

        (i) the relationship between surety and debtor (and the possibility of undue influence) was known to the creditor;

        (ii) consent was obtained by undue influence or the wife lacked adequate understanding of nature and effect of the transaction;

        (iii) creditor did not take reasonable steps to ensure that surety had an adequate understanding.

    (c) Rejected by HL since it might lead to banks, etc. being unwilling to accept matrimonial home as security for loans.

7. Doctrine of notice.

    (a) In *O'Brien* Lord Browne-Wilkinson said that the creditor enforcing the surety depends on actual or constructive notice of the wife's equitable right to set the contract aside.

    (b) The wife must show the bank had constructive notice of the undue influence – it is not for the bank to prove it did not (*Barclays Bank v Boulter and Another* (1999)).

    (c) Wives can show a relationship of trust and confidence in their husbands, so qualify under Class 2B, presumed undue influence, since there is a greater risk of husbands taking advantage of wives to secure agreement to surety.

    (d) So this is sufficient to put a creditor on notice if:

        (i) the contract is not prima facie to the wife's advantage; and

(ii) there is a risk the husband has committed a legal or equitable wrong in getting the wife to stand as surety.

(e) It is possible that the principle applies to cohabitees and other relationships (*Avon Finance Co. v Bridges* (1985)).

(f) The creditor cannot enforce the surety unless he takes 'reasonable steps to satisfy himself that the surety entered into the obligation freely and in knowledge of the true facts …', which involves:

(i) personally interviewing a potential surety without the debtor;

(ii) explaining the full extent of the liability;

(iii) fully explaining the risks involved in standing as surety;

(iv) encouraging the surety to seek independent legal advice.

(g) The creditor has no duty to enquire about the nature of the solicitor's advice (*Massey v Midland Bank plc* (1995)).

(h) A creditor may assume the solicitor will act honestly and competently (*Banco Exterior Internacional v Mann & others* (1994)).

(i) A solicitor advising a wife entering into a second mortgage solely for the benefit of her husband may in any case be liable in negligence for failing to advise her on any issue that is central to the transaction, and for failing to consider what is in her best interests in the widest sense (*Kenyon-Brown v Desmond Banks & Co. (*1999)).

(j) The bank need only act as a reasonable, prudent one would do – they need not show unnecessary suspicion (*Woolwich plc v Gomm* (1999)).

(k) So the *O'Brien* requirements are not exhaustive.

8. The rules applicable when a bank tries to enforce its security against a wife claiming that her consent was obtained by the undue influence of her husband are now laid out in *Royal Bank of Scotland v Etridge (No. 2)* (2001).

(a) A bank instructing solicitors to ensure that a wife involved in a transaction that may be procured by the undue influence of the husband is fixed with constructive notice of the undue influence, unless the solicitor properly advised the wife, and should take steps to ensure the wife is fully informed.

(b) The solicitor must be satisfied that the client was free from improper influence and should inform the wife of the nature of the documents, the seriousness of the risk and that she can back out. The bank must obtain confirmation of the advice given by the solicitor, and if the wife was determined to pursue a transaction that was not sensible then the solicitor should cease to represent her and inform the bank of that.

(c) A solicitor can act for both sides unless he knows that this involves a conflict of interest.

9. In *O'Brien* only the part of the charge the wife was unaware of was set aside, but the entire transaction can be set aside (*TSB Bank plc v Camfield* (1995)).

10. Unless a number of subsequent charges are entered into on the basis of undue influence but the first was entered into voluntarily (*Castle Phillips Finance v Piddington* (1995)).

11. Notice can clearly now be an important factor in Class 1 undue influence (*CIBC Mortgages Ltd v Pitt* (1993)).

The effects of pleading undue influence

1. A successful plea makes the contract voidable.

2. It can be avoided subject to the principles of *restitutio in integrum*.

3. But the claimant may be denied an effective remedy if the value of the property has changed (*Cheese v Thomas* (1994)).

5.5 ILLEGALITY

Contracts void by statute
- Wagers – money paid over not recoverable.
- Restrictive trade practices – now see also Articles 81 & 82 EC treaty.

Contracts illegal by statute
Illegal as formed:
- if prohibited then unenforceable (*Re Mahmoud & Ispahani*);
- unless the statute has a different purpose (*Smith v Mawhood*).

Illegal as performed:
- invalid if the illegality relates to the central purpose of the contract (*Hughes v Asset Management*).

Consequences of illegality
Void by common law:
- clause may be severed (*Goldsoll v Goldman*);
- unless impossible (*Attwood v Lamont*).

Void by statute depends on wording of statute.

Illegal by statute or common law:
- illegal as formed then unenforceable;
- illegally performed – a party not at fault may recover money paid.

ILLEGALITY

Contracts void by common law
Contracts to oust the jurisdiction of the courts – except arbitration clauses or directed to a tribunal by Parliament.

Contracts undermining marriage or relinquishing parental responsibility.

Restraints of trade:
- *prima facie* void;
- must be reasonable to be valid;
- can only protect a legitimate interest, e.g. trade secrets (*Forster v Suggett*) or client connection (*Home Counties Dairies v Skilton*);
- must not extend too far geographically or be for too long a period (*Fitch v Dewes*);
- cannot use other means to effect a restraint (*Bull v Pitney Bowes*);
- can apply to vendor restraints (*Nordenfelt v Maxim Nordenfelt*);
- and to employee restraints.

Contracts illegal by common law
Generally illegal on policy grounds, e.g.
- contracts to commit crimes, torts or frauds (*Dann v Curzon*);
- contracts to defraud the revenue (*Napier v The National Business Agency*);
- contracts aimed at corruption in public life (*Parkinson v The College of Ambulance*);
- contracts to promote sexual immorality (*Pearce v Brooks*).

5.5.1 Introduction

1. Illegality, unlike other vitiating factors, is more to do with character of the agreement than defects affecting voluntariness.
2. The area is complex because judges refer to contracts being illegal, void, and unenforceable and some contracts are declared illegal by statute.
3. One of the overriding factors is public policy.
4. There appear to be four loose groupings within the area:
   - contracts declared void by statute;
   - contracts declared illegal by statute;
   - contracts void at common law;
   - contracts illegal at common law.

5.5.2 Contracts void by statute

1. Contracts of wager.
   (a) Defined in *Carlill v Carbolic Smoke Ball Co.* 'two persons mutually agree that one shall win from the other money or other stake upon determination of some event, neither party having an interest in the contract apart from the stake';
   (b) Generally void by the Gaming Act 1845 – can be made but not enforced, and money already passed is not recoverable;
   (c) More recently many types of betting are regulated by statute.
2. Restrictive trade practices:
   (a) contracts to interfere with free competition, including price fixing, quotas etc. were originally *prima facie* void;
   (b) since the Restrictive Trade Practices Act 1976 the Director General of Fair Trading keeps a register of such agreements;
   (c) Articles 81 and 82 EU Treaty control anti-competitive practices.

5.5.3 Contracts illegal by statute

1. A contract can be declared illegal by statute in one of two ways:
- it is illegal to form such a contract – for public policy reasons;
- it is legally formed but becomes illegal in its performance.

2. Contracts illegal as formed.
   (a) Any contract prohibited by a statute is void *ab initio* and unenforceable (*Re Mahmoud & Ispahani* (1921)).
   (b) This is because, as Lord Mansfield said in *Cope v Rowlands* (1836), it is 'a transgression of the positive laws of the country'.
   (c) If statute has another purpose than to invalidate the contract then the court gives effect to it (*Smith v Mawhood* (1845)).

3. Contracts illegal in the manner of their performance.
   (a) A contract may be legally formed but become illegal because of how it is carried out (*Anderson Ltd. v Daniel* (1924)).
   (b) The contract may again have a different purpose than to render the contract illegal (*Shaw v Groom* (1970)).
   (c) The contract is not automatically unenforceable merely because it is not carried out in the proscribed manner (*St. John Shipping Corporation v Joseph Rank Ltd.* (1956)).
   (d) Illegal performance must relate to the central purpose of the contract (*Hughes v Asset Managers plc* (1995)).

5.5.4 Contracts void at common law

Contracts ousting the jurisdiction of the courts

1. Originally any clause stating that a dispute over the contract should be resolved elsewhere than in court is void – even if there is no other appropriate court there is the supervisory role of the Queen's Bench Division of the High Court.

2. However, courts have accepted arbitration clauses.

3. Parliament in any case directs certain issues away from the courts into, for example, tribunals.

Contracts undermining the institution of marriage

1. Courts traditionally have seen marriage as a sacred institution.
2. So any arrangement that might prejudice a marriage is void.
3. This applies to preventing a marriage or procuring a marriage.

Contracts to relinquish parental responsibility
1. Traditionally parents were prevented from, for example, selling their child.
2. Now rules on surrogacy have complicated the principle.

Contracts in restraint of trade

1. These are arrangements by which one party agrees to limit his/her legal right to carry out a trade, business or profession.
2. Always viewed as *prima facie* void for two reasons:
   - to prevent people from signing away their livelihoods at the request of a party with stronger bargaining power;
   - to avoid depriving the public of the person's expertise.
3. They are of three possible types:
   - employee restraints – to prevent an employee from unfair competition on leaving the employment;
   - vendor restraints – preventing the seller of a business from unfairly competing with the purchaser;
   - agreements of mutual regulation between businesses.
4. These agreements might be upheld as reasonable:
   - as between the parties – so the restraint must be no wider than to protect a legitimate interest;
   - in the public interest – so the restraint must not unduly limit public choice.
5. The reasonableness of the restraint is also measured against factors such as duration and geographical extent.
6. Employee restraints.
   (a) An employer can legitimately protect trade secrets and client connection, but not merely prevent the employee from exercising his/her trade or skill.

(b) So reasonableness is measured against certain criteria.

    (i) A restraint in a highly specialised business is more likely to be reasonable (*Forster & Sons Ltd. v Suggett* (1918)).

    (ii) Restraint of an employee in a key position is more likely to be reasonable (*Morris Ltd. v Saxelby* (1916)).

    (iii) The duration of the extent must not be too long (*Home Counties Dairies Ltd. v Skilton* (1970)).

    (iv) The geographical extent must not be too wide (*Fitch v Dewes* (1921)).

    (v) Similarly, the range of activities that the restraint covers must be no wider than is necessary to protect legitimate interests (*J A Mont (UK) Ltd. v Mills* (1993)).

(c) Soliciting of clients can be prevented by such clauses:

- if not too wide (*M & S Drapers v Reynolds* (1957));
- including clients not within the original scope of the restraint is unreasonable *(Hanover Insurance Brokers Ltd. and Christchurch Insurance Brokers Ltd. v Shapiro* (1994));
- so it is unreasonable to restrain the ex-employee from approaching clients unknown to him/her at the time of employment – compare *Austin Knight (UK) Ltd. v Hinds* (1994) with *G W Plowman & Son Ltd. v Ash* (1964).

(d) Attempting a restraint by other means is also void, including:

- making contractual benefits subject to a restraint (*Bull v Pitney-Bowes Ltd.* (1966));
- agreements between employers (*Kores Manufacturing Co. Ltd. v Kolak Manufacturing Co. Ltd.* (1959));
- restraints in rules of associations (*Eastham v Newcastle United FC Ltd.* (1963)).

7. Vendor restraints.

(a) These are void for public policy both to prevent an individual from negotiating away his/her livelihood, and also because the public may lose a valuable service.

(b) Restraints are more likely to be upheld as reasonable since businesses deal on more equal bargaining strength, even if restraint is very wide (*Nordenfelt v Maxim Nordenfelt Co.* (1894)).

(c) The restraint must still protect a legitimate interest to be valid (*British Concrete Ltd. v Schelff* (1921)).

8. Agreements between merchants, manufacturers or other trades.

(a) If the object is regulation of trade then they are void unless both sides benefit (*English Hop Growers v Dering* (1928)).

(b) So they are void when the parties have unequal bargaining strength (*Schroder Publishing Co. Ltd. v Macaulay* (1974)).

(c) 'Solus' agreements are also void as they act as restraints (*Esso Petroleum. v Harper's Garage (Stourport)* (1968)).

5.5.5 Contracts illegal at common law

1. This is a wide group – the common factor is that the agreement prejudices freedom of contract, so is harmful to the public.

2. In fact, many categories seem to be based on morality.

3. The specific types of agreement include:

* a contract to commit a crime, tort or fraud (*Dann v Curzon* (1911) and *Allen v Rescous* (1677)); or benefit from the crime of another (*Beresford v Royal Insurance Co. Ltd.* (1937));

* a contract to defraud the revenue (*Napier v National Business Agency Ltd.* (1951));

* or to defraud a local authority (*Alexander v Rayson* (1936));

* a contract aimed at corruption in public life (*Parkinson v The College of Ambulance* (1951));

* contracts in breach of foreign law (*Foster v Driscoll* (1929));

* or interfering with justice (*Kearley v Thompson* (1890) and (*Harmony Shipping Co. SA v Davis* (1979)), so there can be no enforceable payment to a police informer (*Carnduff v Rock* (2001));

* contracts to deny a legal right (*Cooper v Willis* (1906) and *Hyman v Hyman* (1929));

- contracts of maintenance (*Martell v Consett Iron Co. Ltd.* (1955)); and of champerty (*Picton Jones & Co. v Arcadia Developments* (1989));
- contracts aimed at promoting sexual immorality (*Pearce v Brooks* (1866) and *Benyon v Nettleford* (1850));
- although this probably only applies now if the activity also amounts to a crime (*Armhouse Lee Ltd. v Chappell* (1996)).

5.5.6 Consequences if a contract declared void

1. The important difference is between common law and statute.
2. Contracts void at common law.
   (a) All of the contract need not be void, only the offending clause.
   (b) So the contract may be severed to remove the offending part (*Goldsoll v Goldman* (1915)).
   (c) This does not apply if the offending part forms main part of the contract, then severance is impossible (*Bennett v Bennett* (1952)).
   (d) Severance is also impossible if it would alter the meaning of the agreement (*Attwood v Lamont* (1920)).
   (e) Severance will not be allowed to defeat public policy (*Napier v National Business Agency Ltd.* (1951)).
   (f) It is possible that money paid over is recoverable (*Hermann v Charlesworth* (1905)).
3. Contracts void by statute.
   (a) The effect depends on what the statute provides.
   (b) In the absence of express wording, common law rules apply.

5.5.7 Consequences if a contract declared illegal

1. Here the difference is between contracts illegal as formed and contracts illegal as performed.

2. Illegal as formed.

(a) The contract is illegal from the start so never becomes legal.

(b) So unenforceable by the parties (*Pearce v Brooks* (1866)).

(c) Property transferred in advance is generally unrecoverable (*Parkinson v The College of Ambulance* (1951)).

(d) This applies even if the parties are unaware of the illegality (*J W Allen (Merchandising) Ltd. v Cloke* (1960)).

(e) Property already handed over is sometimes recoverable if:

   (i) not to allow recovery is an 'affront to public conscience' (*Howard v Shirlstar Container Transport Ltd.* (1990));

   (ii) illegality is not vital to the cause (*Tinsley v Milligan* (1993));

   (iii) the party seeking recovery is not *in pari delicto*, i.e. is not culpable (*Kirri Cotton Co. Ltd. v Dewani* (1960));

   (iv) the agreement has been induced by a fraud (*Hughes v Liverpool Victoria Friendly Society* (1916));

   (v) a party repents before the contract is performed (*Kearley v Thompson* (1890)).

3. Illegal as performed.

(a) If both parties are at fault for the illegal performance then the rule is the same as for illegally formed contracts.

(b) A party who is unaware of the illegality may have remedies, including recovery of money (*Marles v Trant* (1954)), especially where the illegality is only ancillary to the subject of the claim (*Hall v Woolston Hall Leisure Ltd* (2000)).

CHAPTER 6

DISCHARGE OF A CONTRACT

6.1 DISCHARGE OF THE CONTRACT

1. Discharge refers to the point where the contract is ended.
2. This should be when all obligations are satisfactorily performed.
3. However, in some circumstances not all obligations are performed but the contract is still considered to be discharged.
4. When the contract is breached by one party the other party can consider their obligations discharged, and the party breaching the contract is then bound by new 'secondary obligations'.

The basic rule
- Contract not discharged and no payment is enforceable until all obligations are performed.
- Applies in 'entire contracts' (*Cutter v Powell*).
- Also applies to ancillary obligations (*Re Moore & Co and Landauer*).

DISCHARGE BY PERFORMANCE

Avoiding the strict rule
- If the contract is 'divisible', payment for each separate part may be enforceable (*Taylor v Webb*).
- If a party accepts part performance it should be paid for if it was a genuine acceptance (*Sumpter v Hedges*).
- If the contract was substantially performed payment is recoverable (*Dakin v Lee*):
  a) payment in this case is for the part performed (*Hoenig v Isaacs*);
  b) what is 'substantial' is a question of fact (*Bolton v Mahadeva*).
- If a party is prevented from performing, the price is payable (*Planche v Colborn*).
- If a party offers to perform and is refused by the other party then payment is recoverable (*Startup v MacDonald*).

Stipulations as to time of performance
- Stipulations as to time of performance are warranties not conditions.
- But there are three exceptions to this general rule – where time is 'of the essence':
  a) the contract stipulates that time of performance is a condition;
  b) the nature of the contract or its surrounding circumstances mean that time of performance is critical, e.g. sale of perishables;
  c) a party has already failed to perform and the other party then gives a reasonable time to perform.

6.2 DISCHARGE BY PERFORMANCE

6.2.1 The strict rule of performance

1. The strict rule is that a contract is not discharged until all of the obligations have been performed.
2. Generally, a failure to perform an obligation by one party then gives rise to a remedy for the other party.
3. There is, however, no obligation on a party to exceed the standard of performance required by the contract (*Ateni Maritime Corporation v Great Marine* (1991)).
4. The rule originated for 'entire contracts', which require complete performance of all obligations (*Cutter v Powell* (1795)), so part performance only means no payment.
5. The principle applies in Sale of Goods contracts, e.g.:

   * for breaches of the implied condition that goods should be as described under s13 on the basis that 'a ton does not mean about a ton, or a yard about a yard. If a seller wants a margin he must, and in my experience does, stipulate for it' – Lord Atkin in *Arcos Ltd. v Ronaasen* (1933);
   * and this has been extended to include ancillary matters (*Re Moore & Co and Landauer & Co.* (1921));
   * and is now incorporated by a new s30(2A) inserted by s4(2) Sale and Supply of Goods Act 1994.

6. But the strict rule is capable of creating injustice.

6.2.2 Ways of avoiding the strict rule

1. Judges have developed exceptions to avoid injustice.
2. They include part performance or if performance is prevented.

   (a) If the contract has divisible obligations a fair payment can be expected for a part completely performed, and the whole contract is not breached (*Taylor v Webb* (1937)).
   (b) If part performance is accepted by the other side payment for this part should be enforceable unless the acceptance was not genuine (*Sumpter v Hedges* (1898)).

(c) Where performance is substantial then recovery should be possible (*Dakin & Co. v Lee* (1916)).

  (i) The amount payable will correspond to the price of the work less the cost of the incomplete part (*Hoenig v Isaacs* (1952)).

  (ii) What amounts to 'substantial' performance and what is a breach of the whole contract is a question of fact in each case (*Bolton v Mahadeva* (1972)).

(d) If a party is prevented from performing by the other party then the strict rule cannot apply (*Planche v Colborn* (1831)).

(e) Similarly, if a party has tendered performance which has been refused by the other side then that party's obligations are discharged (*Startup v MacDonald* (1843)).

6.2.3 Stipulations as to time of performance

1. Traditionally, failure to perform on the due date is breach of warranty entitling an action for damages but not repudiation.
2. However, in three situations time is said to be 'of the essence', in which case a breach can allow repudiation by the other party:

  • if the parties expressly stipulate in the contract that time is of the essence and identify the possible remedy for repudiation;
  • if the character of the contract or subject matter show that time of performance is critical, e.g. sale of perishable goods;
  • if one party fails to perform and the other party then gives him/her a reasonable time to perform or (s)he will repudiate his/her own obligations.

6.3 DISCHARGE BY AGREEMENT

6.3.1 Introduction

1. If a contract can be made by agreement it can also be ended
2. There are two different types of agreement: bilateral and unilateral.
3. There are two potential problems: lack of consideration and lack of form.

6.3.2 Bilateral agreements

1. If consideration is wholly executory there is no problem ending the contract, as the promise of each party to release the other from performing is good consideration.
2. If consideration is partly or wholly executed at new agreement:
   (a) a party may 'waive' rights (an example of where waiver has followed business practice);
   (b) the clear problem is the absence of consideration – judges will allow waiver to avoid broken promises.
3. If form is an issue:
   (a) traditionally there is no problem with an oral agreement to discharge where s40 LPA was complied with;
   (b) agreements to vary terms are invalid unless evidenced in writing;
   (c) if a new agreement is to be substituted for an existing agreement then it is unenforceable except in writing.

6.3.3 Unilateral discharges

There are two possibilities if one party fails to perform.
1. One party releases the other from performance:
   (a) must be by deed to be valid or fails for lack of consideration;
   (b) the principle may not survive (*Williams v Roffey* (1990)), where the consideration is the 'extra benefit' gained by the party releasing the other from his/her obligations.
2. Accord and satisfaction:
   (a) can be introducing a new element (*British Russian Gazette v Associated Ltd. Newspapers Ltd.* (1933));
   (b) or part payment at an earlier stage (*Pinnel's case*);
   (c) or estoppel, when equity will not allow the party waiving rights to break the promise.

6.4 DISCHARGE BY FRUSTRATION

Types of frustrating event

Impossibility:
- by destruction of the subject matter (*Taylor v Caldwell*);
- by death or illness of a party to the contract (*Condor v The Baron Knights*);
- unavoidable delay (*The Evia*);
- outbreak of war (*Metropolitan Water Board v Dick, Kerr & Co.*).

Subsequent illegality:
- e.g. of another country's laws (*Re Shipton v Anderson*).

Commercial sterility:
- where the main purpose of the contract is gone (*Krell v Henry*);
- unless substantial purpose remains (*Hutton v Herne Bay Steamboat Co.*).

Limitations on the doctrine
- self-induced frustration (*Maritime National Fish Ltd. v Ocean Trawlers Ltd.*).
- Contract becomes more onerous to perform (*Davis Contractors Ltd. v Fareham UDC.*).
- Frustrating event could have been foreseen (*Amalgamated Investment & Property Co. v John Walker & Sons*).
- Frustrating event provided for (*The Fibrosa case*).
- Absolute undertaking to perform (*Paradine v Jane*).

FRUSTRATION

Common law effects of frustration
- Obligations end on frustrating event (*Taylor v Caldwell*).
- But originally still bound by prior obligations (*Chandler v Webster*).
- But can recover if total failure of consideration (*The Fibrosa case*).

Statutory effects of frustration
- Money paid in advance of the contract is recoverable.
- Court can reward a party who has done work under the contract.
- A party can recover for a partial performance that confers a benefit on the other party (*B P Exploration Co. v Hunt*).

6.4.1 The purpose and development of the doctrine

1. Discharge ultimately requires performance of obligations.
2. The traditional rule was that complete performance was required of a party regardless of the reason for the failure to perform (*Paradine v Jane* (1647)).
3. This was unfair if failure to perform was beyond a party's control.
4. So a doctrine developed whereby obligations under the contract ended at the moment the intervening event prevented performance – the doctrine of frustration.
5. Blackburn J expressed it in *Taylor v Caldwell* (1863): 'in contracts which depend on the continued existence of a given person or thing, a condition is implied that the impossibility of performance arising from the perishing of the person or thing shall excuse the performance'.
6. The rule is justified 'because the circumstances in which performance is called for would render it a thing radically different from that which was undertaken by the contract' – Lord Radcliffe in *Davis Contractors Ltd. v Fareham UDC* (1956).
7. The immediate consequences are:
   - both parties are relieved further performance;
   - which does not remove all injustice since the party ready to perform will still be denied performance by the other side;
   - and a number of limitations are placed on the doctrine.

6.4.2 The different types of frustrating events

There are three types of circumstance leading to frustration.

1. Impossibility – one of a number of events meaning that it is no longer possible to perform the contract:
   - the subject matter of the contract has been destroyed (*Taylor v Caldwell* (1863));
   - the subject matter of the contract is not available (*Jackson v Union Marine Insurance Co. Ltd.* (1873));

- one party is unavailable through death or illness (*Robinson v Davison* (1871));
- a party is at risk of being unable to complete performance (*Condor v The Baron Knights* (1966));
- any other good reason prevents a party from being available (*Morgan v Manser* (1948));
- excessive, unavoidable delay (*The Evia; The Wenjiang; Finelvet AG v Vinava Shipping Co. Ltd.* (1983));
- outbreak of war (*Metropolitan Water Board v Dick, Kerr & Co. Ltd.* (1918)).

2. Subsequent illegality – the parties are ready to perform but changes in the law prevent it:
   - the law of another country changes (*Denny, Mott & Dickson v James B Fraser & Co. Ltd.* (1944));
   - law changes because of outbreak of war (*Re Shipton Anderson* (1915)).

3. Commercial sterility – the central purpose of the contract is destroyed by the frustrating event:
   (a) all commercial purpose of the contract is destroyed (*Krell v Henry* (1903));
   (b) all commercial purpose must be gone – if a commercial purpose remains then the contract continues (*Herne Bay Steamboat Co. v Hutton* (1903));
   (c) traditionally frustration could not apply to leases (*Cricklewood Property & Investment Trust Ltd. v Leighton's Investment Trust Ltd.* (1945));
   (d) The House of Lords have since accepted that frustration can apply to leases because they are 'a subsidiary means to an end not an end in themselves' (*National Carriers Ltd. v Panalpina Ltd.* (1981)).

6.4.3 The limitations on the doctrine of frustration

1. The doctrine was developed to prevent the unfairness arising from the requirement to perform in impossible circumstances.

2. It can still be unfair to one party, so courts have identified situations where the doctrine does not apply and the contractual obligations remain:

- where the frustration is self-induced (*Maritime National Fish Ltd. v Ocean Trawlers Ltd.* (1935)), (*J Lauritzen AS v Wijsmuller BV* (1990));
- where the contract is merely more onerous to perform or does not produce the same benefit for a party (*Davis Contractors Ltd. v Fareham UDC* (1956));
- where the parties could have reasonably contemplated the frustrating event (*Amalgamated Investment & Property Co. Ltd. v John Walker & Sons* (1976));
- where the frustrating event was provided for in the contract (*Fibrosa Spolka Akcyjna v Fairbairn Lawson Combe Barbour Ltd. (The Fibrosa case)* (1943)). However, if a 'force majeure' clause does not cover the extent of the damage then a claim of frustration might succeed (*Jackson v Union Marine Insurance Co. Ltd.* (1874));
- where the contract provides for an absolute undertaking to perform (*Paradine v Jane* (1647)).

6.4.4 The common law effects of frustration

1. In the original rule the contract ends at the point of frustration:

- so parties were relieved further performance from this point;
- but would be bound by obligations that arose before the point of frustration (*Chandler v Webster* (1904)).

2. This was unsatisfactory because the effect on the parties was unpredictable depending entirely on what point the parties had reached in the contract when the frustrating event occurred.

3. (a) This basic principle was later overruled by HL in *Fibrosa*, where they held that a party could recover payments made in advance of a contract if there was a total failure of consideration.

   (b) However, this still meant that the other party could be unfairly treated if they had completed work under the contract.

6.4.5 Statutory intervention and the Law Reform (Frustrated Contracts) Act 1943

1. The doctrine developed in response to hardships caused by *Paradine v Jayne*; nevertheless it in turn created injustices.

2. As a result the Act was passed specifically to mitigate some of the harshness of the common law.

3. The Act deals with three very specific areas:

    (a) recovery of money already paid in advance of the contract:

        (i) S1(2) confirms the principle, developed in *Fibrosa*, that money already paid over is recoverable;

        (ii) as with the basic rule in *Taylor v Caldwell*, money due ceases to be payable;

    (b) under s1(2) the court also has a discretion to reward a party who has carried out work under the contract;

    (c) recovery for partial performance:

        ● under s1(3) the court can allow recovery for partial performance which has conferred a valuable benefit on the other party;

        ● this is at the discretion of the court to determine what is reasonable in the circumstances (*BP Exploration Co. (Libya) Ltd. v Hunt (No. 2) (1979)*).

4. In certain circumstances operation of the Act is excluded:

● contracts for the carriage of goods by sea, except for time charter parties;

● contracts of insurance (which in any case are based on acceptance of risks);

● perishing of goods under the Sale of Goods Act 1979.

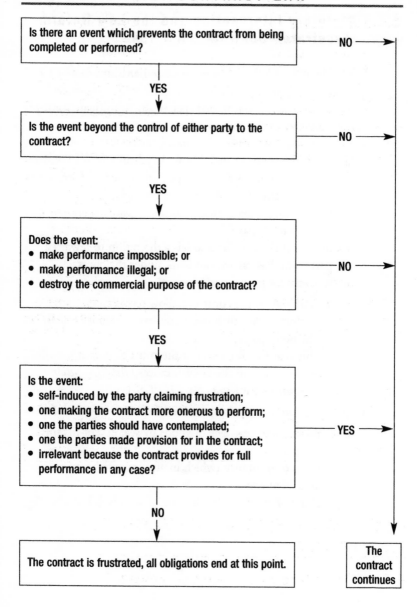

When a contract will be considered frustrated

The nature of breach

Breach occurs where a party either:
- fails to perform obligations;
- fails to achieve the standards set in the contract;
- repudiates obligations unlawfully.

Lord Diplock explained in *Photo Productions* that a contract is made up of 'primary' obligations which, if breached, are replaced by 'secondary' obligations, e.g. to pay damages.

Types of breach

Breach of a term generally:
- can be any type – condition, warranty, or innominate;
- and damages are always available.

Breach of a condition:
- can be expressed by the parties or implied by fact or law;
- but must act as a condition to achieve the full range of remedies (*Schuler v Wickman*);
- could be innominate where the breach is sufficiently serious to destroy the purpose of the contract (*The Hong Kong Fir case*).

Anticipatory breach:
- where a party indicates a future breach. Can be either intending not to perform, or not in the proscribed manner.

BREACH

Consequences of breach

Breach of a term:
- an action for damages is always available;
- and is the only remedy for breach of warranty.

Breach of a condition:
- can sue for damages and/or repudiate.

Anticipatory breach:
- can sue immediately (*Frost v Knight*);
- or wait until the contract date (*Avery v Bowden*).

6.5 DISCHARGE BY BREACH OF CONTRACT

6.5.1 The nature of a breach of contract

1. A breach occurs if a party fails to perform contractual obligations.

2. This can occur in one of three ways:

- failure to perform an obligation;
- failure to match quality of performance required by contract;
- repudiating obligations unlawfully, i.e. without justification.

3. Calling failure to perform obligations a discharge of them seems somewhat illogical. Lord Diplock explained the position in *Photo Productions Ltd v Securicor Transport Ltd.* (1980):

- the original contractual obligations are 'primary' obligations;
- on breach these obligations are replaced (rather than discharged) by secondary obligations, e.g. to pay damages.

4. He also identified two basic exceptions to this rule:

- 'fundamental breach' – if a party breaches a fundamental term (one depriving the other party of the major benefit they expected under the contract) the whole contract is breached;
- breach of a condition – where the term is so central to the contract that failure to perform makes it meaningless.

5. The difference between these two traditionally was that an exclusion clause could not be relied upon in a fundamental breach, but exclusion of liability for a condition could succeed.

6.5.2 The different types of breach

1. There are three identifiable types of breach.

2. Breach of a term generally.

- Here it does not matter how the term is classified.
- It might include a minor breach of an innominate term.
- On breach there is always an action for damages available.

3. Breach of a condition.

- A condition can either be expressed by the parties or implied by fact or law.
- To produce the full range of remedies it must, however, conform to the proper description of a condition (*Schuler v Wickman Machine Tool Sales Ltd.* (1973)).
- It might also include an innominate term where the breach was sufficiently serious to warrant repudiation by the other

party (*The Hong Kong Fir case* (1962)).

- It might include fundamental breach.

4. Anticipatory breach.

- This occurs if one party notifies the other party of intention to breach the contract – so more accurately described as breach by anticipatory repudiation (*Hochester v De La Tour* (1853)).
- Not all terms need to be breached, and it may merely refer to performance other than in the proscribed manner.

6.5.3 The consequences of breach

1. The consequences of breach can vary with the type of breach.
2. Breach of a term generally:

- an action for damages is always available;
- with a warranty only an action for damages is available and any attempt to repudiate obligations will be a breach.

3. Breach of a condition:

- the party can sue for damages and/or repudiate obligations;
- before repudiating the party must be sure that the term is a condition or there is a sufficiently serious breach, otherwise that repudiation may be a breach (*Cehave NV v Bremen Handelsgesellschaft mbH (The Hansa Nord)* (1975)).

4. Anticipatory breach.

- Here the victim of the breach may treat the contract as at an end and sue immediately (*Frost v Knight* (1872)).
- Alternatively, the party may wait until performance is actually due and remains unperformed (*Avery v Bowden* (1855)).
- This may, however, leave that party without a remedy if (s)he becomes liable for a later breach (*Fercometal SARL v Mediterranean Shipping Co. SA* (1988)).
- An anticipatory breach can also arise if a party mistakenly treats an anticipatory breach as an actual breach and then treats the contract as having ended (*Federal Commerce and Navigation Co. Ltd. v Molena Alpha Inc.* (1979)).

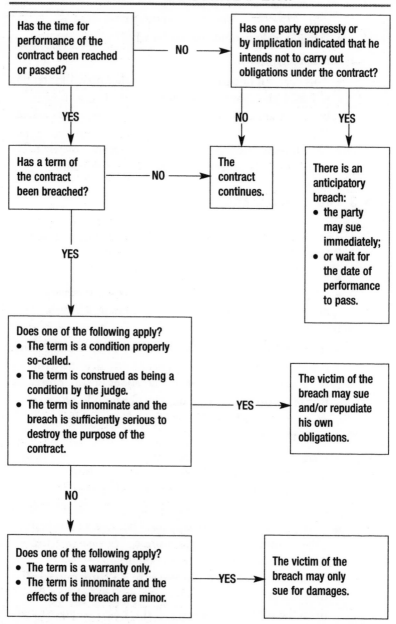

The consequences of different types of breach of contract

Causation and remoteness of damage

- Breach must be the main reason for the claimant's loss (*London Joint Stock Bank v MacMillan*).
- There are two types of loss for which the claimant can recover – (i) natural consequence of the breach; (ii) that in the contemplation of parties at time contract formed (*Hadley v Baxendale*).
- Can only recover for what is foreseeable (*Victoria Laundry v Newman Industries*).

Bases of assessment
Three normal bases.

- Loss of bargain – e.g. loss of profit, or failure to deliver – can be subject to 'the available market rule' (compare *Charter v Sullivan* and *Thompson v Robinson Gunmakers*).
- Reliance loss, i.e. necessary expenses made in advance of contract (*Anglia TV v Reed*).
- Restitution, i.e. a price already paid under the contract.

Mental distress
Possible for claimant and his/her family in holiday cases (*Jarvis v Swan Tours*) and (*Jackson v Horizon Holidays*).

DAMAGES

Quantum meruit
For services already rendered if:

- contract silent on payment (*Powell v Upton RDC*);
- fresh agreement should be implied (*Steven v Bromley*);
- further performance prevented (*De Barnady v Harding*).

Liquidated damages
Identified in the contract itself. Must not be a penalty.
Test in *Dunlop v New Garage*:

- extravagant sum is a penalty;
- payment of a large sum for a small debt is a penalty;
- one sum for a variety of breaches is a penalty, a sum for one breach is not;
- wording used by parties not conclusive, but construction by court;
- a claim for liquidated damages will not fail because potential loss was impossible to calculate at the time of formation.

CHAPTER 7

REMEDIES

7.1 COMMON LAW REMEDIES

7.1.1 Introduction

1. The most common remedy for breach of contract is damages – a sum of money in compensation – a common law remedy.
2. It is artificial and nothing to do with enforcing the contract. As a result of its shortcomings other remedies developed in equity.
3. If a case is proven in common law, damages are automatically granted – equitable remedies are at the discretion of the court.
4. While a claimant must state in the pleadings which remedy is required, both types of remedy can be granted at the same time.
5. There are three types of compensation available at common law:
   - a sum of unliquidated damages based on the precise loss;
   - a liquidated sum fixed by the parties at the time the contract was formed;
   - a *quantum meruit* for a partly performed contract of service based on an amount representing the work already done.

7.1.2 Unliquidated damages

1. Contract damages are to 'put the victim of the breach, so far as is possible and so far as the law allows, into the position he would have been in if the contract had not been broken' – Parke B in *Robinson v Harman* (1848).
2. Nominal damages are possible even if no actual loss is suffered.

3. There are two tests establishing exactly what a party will recover:

- one to determine the type of loss for which the claimant can recover – based on causation and remoteness of damage;
- one to establish the amount recoverable in respect of the actual loss – called the bases of assessment.

7.1.3 Tests of causation and remoteness of damage

1. Here there are two key questions.

- Is there a causal link between the defendant's breach and the actual damage or loss suffered by the claimant?
- Is the damage of a type that is not too remote a consequence of the defendant's breach?

2. Causation.

(a) Causation is a question of fact in each case – the court decides if the breach is the main reason for the claimant's loss (*London Joint Stock Bank v MacMillan* (1918)).

(b) The test is a common sense one of whether the breach was the cause or merely the occasion of the loss (*Galoo Ltd. and Others v Bright Grahame Murray* (1995)).

(c) The loss may be the result of the character of the contract itself rather than any breach, in which case the defendant is not liable (*C & P Haulage v Middleton* (1983)).

(d) The loss may arise partly from the breach and partly from an intervening event (*Stansbie v Troman* (1948)).

- In cases such as this the chain of causation is not broken if it is a reasonably foreseeable event (*De La Bere v Pearson* (1908)).
- If there are two causal factors, including the breach, then the loss can still be attributed to the breach (*Smith, Hogg & Co. v Black Sea Insurance* (1940)).

3. Remoteness of damage.

(a) Alderson B said damages should be for losses 'such as may fairly and reasonably be considered arising either naturally, i.e. according to the usual course of things, for such breach of contract itself, or such as may be reasonably supposed to have been in the contemplation of both parties at the time they made the contract.' (*Hadley v Baxendale* (1854)).

(b) So there are two possible types of recoverable loss:

  ● a natural consequence of the breach – measured objectively;

  ● a loss which, if not a natural consequence, the parties knew was possible when they contracted – measured subjectively.

(c) This has since been modified by Asquith LJ in *Victoria Laundry Ltd. v Newman Industries Ltd.* (1949) to include six vital points:

  ● to indemnify any loss is too harsh on the defendant;

  ● recoverable loss should be measured against foreseeability;

  ● foresight depends on knowledge of parties when contracting;

  ● knowledge is of two types: (i) imputed knowledge, i.e. common knowledge; and (ii) actual knowledge, i.e. that actually possessed by the parties on formation of the contract (these represent the two types identified in *Hadley v Baxendale*);

  ● but knowledge can also be implied from what a reasonable man might have contemplated;

  ● implied knowledge should include what it is possible to have foreseen rather than what must have been foreseen.

(d) The test can cause confusion. The House of Lords added to the confusion in *Koufos v C Czarnikow Ltd. (The Heron II)* (1969), where it held: (i) often the reasonable man ought to contemplate certain loss as a natural consequence of a breach; and (ii) foresight is different in contract and tort.

(e) This was rejected by the Court of Appeal in *H Parsons (Livestock) Ltd. v Uttley Ingham* (1978), holding that remoteness is not dependent on contemplation of possible level of injury, but merely proof loss could be contemplated.

7.1.4 The bases of assessment

1. If no loss is suffered but a breach is proved, e.g. to declare a contract ended, then nominal damages can be granted (*Staniforth v Lyall* (1830)).
2. There are three normal bases of assessment.
   (a) Loss of a bargain – which puts the party in the position as if the contract had been properly performed. It includes:
      ● where goods or services are defective, the difference between the contract quality and the quality received (*Bence Graphics International Ltd. v Fasson UK Ltd.* (1996));
      ● in a failure to deliver goods or a refusal to accept delivery, the difference between the contract price and that in an 'available market', i.e. if the claimant can get the goods or sell the goods for the same price, or even make a better bargain, then there is no entitlement to damages (*Charter v Sullivan* (1957)). However, if the claimant must pay more to get the goods or cannot get rid of the goods because there is no available market, then recovery is possible (*W L Thompson Ltd. v Robinson Gunmakers Ltd.* (1955));
      ● loss of profit;
      ● loss of a chance. In *Chaplin v Hicks* (1911), an actress recovered in respect of an audition she was prevented from attending when 50 people were to audition. This does not apply if the claimant just takes advantage of the defendant's breach (*Pilkington v Wood* (1953)).
   (b) Reliance loss.
      ● recovery of the expenses that the claimant has necessarily incurred in advance of the contract being performed;
      ● which is normally claimed when any loss of profit is too speculative (*Anglia Television v Reed* (1972));
      ● usually impossible to recover both loss of a bargain and reliance loss since it is compensating twice for the same loss;

- but recovery of both is possible if the loss of a bargain claim covers only net rather than gross profit (*Western Web Offset Printers Ltd. v Independent Media Ltd.* (1995)).

(c) Restitution – this is a simple repayment of any of the price already paid over by the claimant.

7.1.5 The duty to mitigate

1. A claimant has a duty to take 'all reasonable steps to mitigate the loss consequent on the breach' which then 'debars him from claiming in respect of any part of the damage which is due to his neglect to take such steps'. Lord Haldane in *British Westinghouse Electric and Manufacturing Co. Ltd. v Underground Electric Railways Co. of London Ltd.* (1912).

2. The claimant must not take any unreasonable steps that would increase the loss (*The Borag* (1981)).

3. However, the claimant is not bound to take extraordinary steps to mitigate the loss (*Pilkington v Wood* (1953)).

4. In an anticipatory breach the claimant need not terminate at once to mitigate the loss, but can wait until the actual breach (*White and Carter v McGregor* (1962)).

7.1.6 The 'mental distress' cases

1. Traditionally judges would not allow recovery of compensation that would be more appropriately claimed in a tort action:

   (a) so a claim for injury to reputation and consequent mental distress failed in *Addis v The Gramophone Co.* (1909);

   (b) as did a claim for indignity in *Hurst v Picture Theatres* (1913).

2. More recently judges have given damages for mental distress in certain limited circumstances in the so-called 'holiday cases':

   - loss of enjoyment and inconvenience caused by double booking (*Cook v Spanish Holidays* (1960));

- mental distress caused by a total failure to match the description given (*Jarvis v Swan Tours* (1973));
- mental distress caused to the claimant's family (despite inconsistency with privity) in *Jackson v Horizon Holidays* (1975) 'the provision of comfort, pleasure, and 'peace of mind' was a central feature of the contract'.

3. The principle only applies to the holiday cases and is not appropriate to commercial contracts (*Woodar Investment Development Ltd. v Wimpey Construction UK Ltd.* (1980)).

4. It has been extended to failures by solicitors (*Heywood v Wellers (1976)* and *Hayes v James and Charles Dodd* (1990)).

5. More recently damages have been awarded for 'loss of amenity' where the sole purpose of the contract was 'the provision of a pleasurable amenity' (*Ruxley Electronics and Construction Ltd. v Forsyth: Laddingford Enclosures Ltd. v Forsyth* (1995)), and sometimes even where the valuable amenity is not purely pleasurable (*Farley v Skinner* (2001)).

7.1.7 Liquidated damage clauses

1. These apply where parties fix in advance in the contract the sum of damages payable in the event of a breach.

2. The court will only enforce the sum identified where it represents a proper assessment of the loss.

3. There are two possibilities:
   - the sum fixed in the contract is declared valid and no further claim for unliquidated damages is then possible;
   - the sum in the contract is seen as a 'penalty', i.e. it does not relate to the actual loss – in this case a claim for unliquidated damages is possible.

4. Wherever a clause provides for a greater sum than the actual loss it is *prima facie* void, and the party claiming it must prove that it is not a penalty in order to succeed in the claim (*Bridge v Campbell Discount Co.* (1962)).

5. In *Dunlop Pneumatic Tyre Co. v New Garage & Motor Co.*
(1914), Lord Dunedin established a test for differentiating
between genuine liquidated damages and penalties:

- an extravagant sum is generally a penalty;
- payment of a large sum for default on a small debt is most
  likely a penalty;
- one sum operating for a variety of breaches is likely to be a
  penalty, whereas a sum that relates to a single breach is not;
- the wording used by the parties is not conclusive, it is the
  construction by the court that counts;
- a claim for liquidated damages will not fail because
  potential loss was impossible to calculate at the time of
  formation.

7.1.8 Claims for quantum meruit

1. This is an unqualified sum in respect of services already
   rendered.
2. There are three common circumstances when it is granted:
   - if an express or implied contract for services has no details
     on the amount of payment (*Upton RDC v Powell* (1942));
   - where circumstances show that a fresh agreement should be
     implied in place of the old one (*Steven v Bromley* (1919));
   - if one party elects to discharge his own obligations by the
     other party's breach, or a party is prevented from performing
     – in either case that party may sue for work already done
     under the contract (*De Barnady v Harding* (1853)).

Specific performance
- An order for party in default to carry out obligations under the contract.
- Remedy only granted if:
  a) damages would be inadequate (*Fothergill v Rowlands*);
  b) subject matter is unique (*Adderly v Dixon*);
  c) claimant acts with conscience (*Webster v Cecil*);
  d) no excessive delay in seeking it (*Milward v Earl of Thanet*);
  e) not a contract of personal service (*De Francesco v Barnum*);
  f) would not cause hardship to defendant (*Hope v Walter*);
  g) claimant has performed or is ready to do so (*Dyster v Randall*);
  h) mutuality is possible (*Flight v Bolland*);
  i) court can oversee order – compare *Ryan v Mutual Tontine Westminster Association* and *Posner v Scott-Lewis*.

EQUITABLE REMEDIES

Rectification
An order to redraft a written contract which inaccurately represents the actual agreement (*Webster v Cecil*).

Injunctions
- An order to restrain a party from breaching contractual obligations
- Covers three situations:
  a) enforcing restraint of trade clauses – in which case must (i) protect a legitimate interest, (ii) be reasonable between the parties and in the public interest, (iii) be reasonable in duration and geographical extent (*Fitch v Dewes*);
  b) to protect confidentiality (*Faccenda Chicken v Fowler*);
  c) to enforce compliance with a contract of personal service, in which case: (i) contract must contain express negative provision to that effect (*Warner Bros. v Nelson*), (ii) provision must not merely prevent the person from working (*Lumley v Wagner*), (iii) the provision must not be futile or unreasonable (*Page One Records v Britton*).

Rescission
- An order putting the parties back to their pre-contractual position.
- So only available if:
  a) *Restitutio in integrum* is possible (*Clarke v Dickson*);
  b) contract is not affirmed (*Long v Lloyd*);
  c) no excessive delay (*Leaf v International Galleries*);
  d) no third party has gained rights (*Oakes v Turquand*);
  e) judge has not declared damages a better remedy under s2(2) Misrepresentation Act 1967.

7.2 EQUITABLE REMEDIES

7.2.1 Introduction

1. Equitable remedies developed at an early stage in the law.
2. They developed because of the deficiencies of the common law and the inadequacies of the common law remedy of damages.
3. There are several equitable remedies operating in different ways.
4. Four in particular are of significance to contract law:
   - specific performance;
   - injunctions;
   - rescission;
   - rectification of a document.
5. Three major points need to be remembered:
   - they are at the discretion of the court, so are not awarded automatically on proof of the action as damages are;
   - they are granted subject to (i) the general maxims of equity, and (ii) individual requirements;
   - they relate to the individual problem suffered by the injured party, so are very useful as remedies.

7.2.2 Specific performance

1. Specific performance is a straightforward order of the court for the party in breach of contract to carry out his/her obligations.
2. It is a difficult remedy for the courts to either enforce or oversee.
3. As a result it is rarely awarded, and is only granted:
   - if the subject matter of the contract is unique and could not be replaced;
   - it is thus impossible to accurately assess damages and damages are thus an inadequate remedy;
   - the injured party is left without an adequate remedy.

4. So it is only granted subject to well-established principles.

  (a) It is never granted if damages is an adequate remedy for the breach (*Fothergill v Rowland* (1873)).

  (b) It is only granted if the subject matter is unique e.g. usually land (*Adderly v Dixon* (1824)); or art objects (*Falcke v Gray* (1859); or sometimes ships (compare *Behnke v Bede Shipping Co. Ltd.* (1927) with *The Stena Nautica (No. 2)* (1982)).

  (c) It will be denied if the claimant has acted unconscionably (*Webster v Cecil* (1861)).

  (d) It will be denied if there is an excessive delay in seeking the remedy (*Milward v Earl of Thanet* (1801)) – although a two-year delay has been held to be acceptable in *Lazard Bros. V Fairfield Properties Co.* (1977).

  (e) It is not usually granted in a contract of employment or for personal services (*De Francesco v Barnum* (1890)), changed somewhat in recent years where an employee is seeking the remedy to prevent the employer breaching the contract and the order is to use the appropriate disciplinary procedure (*Robb v Hammersmith and Fulham* (1991)).

  (f) It will not be granted where to do so causes undue hardship to the defendant (*Hope v Walter* (1900)).

  (g) It will not be granted unless the claimant can show that (s)he has honoured his/her obligations under the contract or is at least ready and willing to do so (*Dyster v Randall* (1926)).

  (h) The remedy depends on mutuality of obligation so it will not be granted where it could not be enforced against the claimant if (s)he was in breach (*Flight v Bolland* (1828)).

  (i) The remedy is also not granted if the court is incapable of overseeing it and ensuring that the remedy is enforced – compare *Ryan v Mutual Tontine Westminster Chambers Association* (1893), with *Posner v Scott-Lewis* (1987).

7.2.3 Injunctions

1. An injunction is an order of the court to insist that a party to a contract complies with an obligation under the contract or is restrained from carrying out a breach of the contract.
2. Injunctions creating positive obligations are called mandatory, and are rare because of the difficulty of overseeing them.
3. Injunctions creating negative obligations or restraints are called prohibitory and these are the most common.
4. Injunctions can be granted *inter partes* or in an *ex parte* hearing.
5. Most commonly injunctions are interlocutory, in advance of the wider issue being tried, but injunctions can be for final relief.
6. Injunctions are sought in three situations in contract law.

    (a) To enforce a clause in restraint of trade.
    - Such contracts are *prima facie* void and so to be enforceable must satisfy a test of reasonableness, as between the parties and in the public interest, and the claimant must have a legitimate interest to protect.
    - A restraint is only enforced by injunction if it is reasonable both in duration and in geographical extent – compare *Fitch v Dewes* (1921) with *Fellowes v Fischer* (1976).

    (b) To restrain a breach of confidence in a contract.
    - This may be in order to protect a trade secret or a secret manufacturing process (*Forster v Suggett* (1918)).
    - Or it may be to protect a client connection or to prevent the solicitation of existing customers (*Faccenda Chicken v Fowler* (1986)).

    (c) To encourage performance of contracts of personal services.
    - To succeed a claimant must show the contract contains an express negative stipulation restraining the other party from taking other employment (*Warner Brothers v Nelson* (1937)).

- The claimant must also show the stipulation does not merely prevent the employee from earning a living (*Lumley v Wagner* (1852)).
- The injunction will not be granted if in itself it is futile or unreasonable (*Page One Records v Britton* (1968)).

7.2.4 Rescission

1. This is an order of the court which seeks to return the parties to their pre-contractual positions if this is possible.
2. So it is claimed by a party who is trying to avoid a contract voidable for some vitiating factor, e.g. misrepresentation or mistake.
3. It is a very precise remedy and, because of its character, important requirements must be met before it is granted.
   (a) *Restitutio in integrum* must be possible, i.e. it must be possible to return the parties to their exact pre-contract situations – if the subject matter has changed significantly then the remedy is refused (*Clark v Dickson* (1858)). However, in some cases precise restitution is not demanded (*Head v Tattersall* (1871)). In *Armstrong v Jackson* (1917), rescission allowed of a contract for shares when the value of the shares dropped from £3 to 25p each.
   (b) The contract must not have been affirmed by the party seeking rescission (*Long v Lloyd* (1958)).
   (c) The remedy is denied if there is too great a delay in seeking it (*Leaf v International Galleries* (1950)).
   (d) The remedy is denied if a third party has subsequently gained rights in the property (*Oakes v Turquand* (1867)).
   (e) If, under s2(2) Misrepresentation Act 1967, the judge deems damages a better remedy then rescission is unavailable.

7.2.5 Rectification of a document

1. This is an order of the court to alter a written contractual document.
2. It will be granted when a written agreement contradicts the actual agreement made by the parties (*Webster v Cecil* (1861)).

INDEX

The law at your fingertips…
with **Key Facts**

Series Editors: Jacqueline Martin and Chris Turner

Key Facts has been specifically written for students studying Law. It is the essential revision tool for a broad range of law courses from A Level to degree level.

The series is written and edited by an expert team of authors whose experience means they know exactly what is required in a revision aid. They include examiners, barristers and lecturers who have brought their expertise and knowledge to the series to make it user-friendly and accessible.

Key features:
- User-friendly layout and style
- Diagrams, charts and tables to illustrate key points
- Summary charts at basic level, followed by more detailed explanations, to aid revision at every level
- Pocket sized and easily portable
- Written by highly regarded authors and editors

The **Key Facts** series includes:

Consumer Law	0 340 88758 3	144pp	£5.99	**NEW**
Contract Law, 2nd edition	0 340 88949 7	144pp	£5.99	**NEW**
Employment Law, 2nd edition	0 340 88947 0	160pp	£5.99	**NEW**
Human Rights	0 340 88696 X	144pp	£5.99	**NEW**
Tort, 2nd edition	0 340 88948 9	144pp	£5.99	**NEW**
Company Law	0 340 84586 4	128pp	£5.99	
Constitutional & Administrative Law	0 340 81272 9	106pp	£5.99	
Criminal Law, 2nd edition	0 340 88605 6	136pp	£5.99	
Equity & Trusts	0 340 87173 3	138pp	£5.99	
European Law	0 340 84584 8	136pp	£5.99	
Evidence	0 340 85935 0	152pp	£5.99	
Family Law	0 340 81474 8	168pp	£5.99	
Land Law, 2nd edition	0 340 81563 9	112pp	£5.99	
The English Legal System	0 340 80179 4	120pp	£5.99	

Visit <u>www.hoddereducation.co.uk</u> for full details on how to order.

Unlocking the Law

Series Editors: Jacqueline Martin and Chris Turner

Unlocking the Law is a completely new series of textbooks
with a unique approach to undergraduate study of law, designed
specifically so that the subject matter is readable and that
students are not overwhelmed with page after page of
continuous prose.

The text of each title is broken up with features and activities
that have been written to ensure that students are pointed in the
right direction when it comes to understanding the purpose of
different areas within the course. All titles in the series follow
the same format and include the same features so that students
can move easily from one law subject to another.

The series covers all the core subjects required by the Bar
Council and the Law Society for entry onto professional
qualifications and will expand to include titles on option areas.

Unlocking the Law includes the following titles:

Unlocking Constitutional & Administrative Law	0 340 81606 6	Publishing May 05
Unlocking Contract Law	0 340 81566 3	Available now
Unlocking Criminal Law	0 340 81565 5	Available now
Unlocking EU Law	0 340 88759 1	Publishing May 05
Unlocking Land Law	0 340 81564 7	Available now
Unlocking Legal Learning	0 340 88761 3	Publishing May 05
Unlocking The English Legal System	0 340 88693 5	Publishing May 05
Unlocking Torts	0 340 81567 1	Available now
Unlocking Trusts	0 340 88694 3	Publishing May 05

Visit www.unlockingthelaw.co.uk or www.hoddereducation.co.uk for full details on how to order.

The English Legal System
4th edition

A brand new edition of the bestselling and hugely popular textbook for A level students.

Jacqueline Martin
0 340 89991 3
May 2005
£14.99

The English Legal System 4th edition is an essential textbook for all students taking an A level in Law.

It covers all the necessary AS level topics in a clear order and accessible language, and uses a range of diagrams, charts and activities to ensure that complex concepts are understood and that students are able to learn and retain the necessary information.

Features include:

- Full coverage in clear units
- Diagrams and illustrations to highlight concepts
- A range of activities with sample answers
- Examination advice and tips

Criminal Law
3rd edition

An excellent textbook for all A Level students studying the Criminal Law option.

Diana Roe
0 340 90047 4
July 2005
£14.99

This third edition of the popular Criminal Law text is the ideal resource for students studying Criminal Law as their A2 option, and for students on other law courses.

The new edition has been fully updated to include all recent changes in the law, and is filled with stimulating resources and exercises for students of all abilities.

Key features include:

- Full coverage of the specification in clear units
- Special chapter devoted to the synoptic units in Module 6
- Diagrams and illustrations to highlight concepts
- Activities to reinforce learning, with sample answers included
- Examination advice and tips
- Real cases and extracts to highlight important areas and bring law to life.